PORTSMOUTH IN THE TWENTIETH CENTURY
A PHOTOGRAPHIC HISTORY

PORTSMOUTH
in the Twentieth Century
A PHOTOGRAPHIC HISTORY

Portsmouth Museums and Records Service

HALSGROVE

First published in 1999 by Halsgrove
Reprinted 2002, 2004
Copyright © 1999 Portsmouth Museums and Records Service

ISBN 1 84114 033 3

British Library Cataloguing-in-Publication-Data
A CIP data record for this book is available from the British Library

---

**DEDICATED TO THE PEOPLE
OF PORTSMOUTH**

HALSGROVE
Halsgrove House
Lower Moor Way
Tiverton EX16 6SS
T: 01884 243242
F: 01884 243325
www.halsgrove.com

Printed and bound in United Kingdom
by CPI Bath Press

Contents

Acknowledgements

All the photographs in this book are from Portsmouth Museums and Records Service's collections or the city's negative archive it administers. Compiling the book would have been impossible without the generosity of the hundreds of people who have given us photographs or allowed us to copy pictures they own, and we would like to express our gratitude to them. Access to the collections can be obtained through the Service's searchroom at the City Museum and Records Office, Museum Road, Portsmouth, which is open Monday to Friday.

The service would like to thank everyone who has helped its staff prepare this book, including the many volunteers who have mounted and catalogued the photographic collections, Roy Beresford and Clive Marshall. Particular thanks are due to Kevin Purdy, of the University of Portsmouth Photographic Section, who copied and printed most of the pictures reproduced here and kindly allowed us to use his aerial photograph of the Gunwharf, and June Long, who printed items from *The News* archive.

The service is grateful to the following people for permission to reproduce pictures for which they hold the copyright: *The News*, Portsmouth; The Imperial War Museum; Mr Michael Richardson; Mrs J. Reynolds; Miss Madge Farrant; Mrs Susan Crockford; Mr D. G. Dine; Mr Danny Weinstein; The University of Portsmouth; J. A. Hewes Ltd; Mr Ron Forrest, Wright & Logan Ltd.

Introduction

As we approach the millennium and look back over the last hundred years, we can see that Portsmouth has altered dramatically in almost every way. The city has undergone change that was wider ranging, more thorough and faster than in any earlier century, and its history, its development, has taken new directions. The photographs reproduced in this book provide some telling evidence of this change, but like other forms of evidence they tell only part of the story.

One of the biggest changes has been in the number of people living in the city. For nearly three centuries, between 1650 and 1939, Portsmouth's population grew. This growth was not steady and there were periods when the town's inhabitants may even have fallen slightly in number, but the trend was inexorably upwards until the Second World War. In 1901 Portsmouth had 189,160 citizens; by 1939 there were estimated to be 260,000 people living in the city. Such growth could not be contained within the town's existing boundaries. In 1904, 1920 and in 1932 they were extended, taking in first the north of Portsea Island, then Cosham, Paulsgrove and Wymering, and finally Drayton and eastern Portchester. New housing went up in these districts, such as the Highbury estate, 'Wymering Garden City' and the bungalows and semis of Drayton. Portsmouth became a city in 1926 and in 1928 its chief citizen received the title 'Lord Mayor'. Then came the war.

The Second World War was a watershed in Portsmouth's history. Thousands of people left Portsmouth during the war, to join the war effort, escape the bombing or because their homes were destroyed and they could not find new ones in the city. Many never returned. The city's population in 1951 had dropped to 233,545, and it continued falling until in 1991 only 177,142 people lived here. The council began in the 1960s to be concerned that the city might cease to be viable as a community, especially as it was younger people who were leaving, causing the age range of the population to be skewed towards the economically less active. It altered its policies, and it is estimated Portsmouth will have 192,000 inhabitants by 2001.

Arguably, however, this population decline was more apparent than real. The population of Portsmouth's satellite and neighbouring communities, Widley, Horndean, Waterlooville, Bedhampton, Portchester and Havant, grew spectacularly after the war, not least because the city was actively exporting people to the new estates it built at Leigh Park, Wecock Farm and Crookhorn. Portsmouth tried to expand its boundaries again in the 1950s, but was not permitted to do so. One result was friction between the city fathers and other local authorities in south-east Hampshire over planning matters.

The fall in population was partly due to Portsmouth's attempts to improve the legacy of housing and poor town planning from the nineteenth century. Portsmouth is still the most densely populated city in Britain, having 17.6 people per acre in 1991, and before 1940 large parts of it were even more crowded than now. This was particularly true of the older areas, in the south-western corner of Portsea Island, where the inhabitants lived mostly in cramped, poorly-built terraced houses rushed up by speculative builders between 1700 and 1850. In Portsea there were as many as 200 people per acre, in Landport 145. Surveys of houses in poor condition for the Medical Officer of Health in the 1920s showed that in these areas many homes were small, some less than only 12 feet (3.5 m) square, in narrow, dingy courtyards behind the main streets, built back-to-back with other houses so there were no rear windows to allow through ventilation, and sharing a cold water tap and toilet with several other houses.

Housing problems on such a scale could only be solved by a central authority with powers of compulsory purchase and the resources to pay for improvements, namely the council. As early as 1910 some two hundred slums were cleared in Portsea to make way for Curzon Howe Road, a street of well-built council houses with bathrooms, outside toilets, water heating arrangements and three bedrooms, one for the parents, one for female children and one for male children. After the First World War more houses were built at Hilsea, Eastney and Wymering, and flats were erected in Portsea. Progress was slow, however, because of the expense and because the new houses on the cleared sites housed fewer families than had been moved out when the slums were demolished. The German bombing of 1940-44, which fell most severely on the most crowded areas of Portsmouth, literally cleared the way for more drastic action. Nearly a tenth of the city's homes were completely destroyed, including all but a few of those identified as unfit for habitation, and almost as many severely damaged. Naturally the existing housing problems were exacerbated, especially as no new houses could be built in wartime.

The city responded vigorously, arguably at the expense of delaying the rebuilding of the blitzed city centre. A structure plan for the postwar city was adopted in 1943. It envisaged the creation of satellite communities on the mainland, while the population of Portsea Island was to be reduced in order to improve living conditions there. Land for these new houses was bought at Leigh Park in 1944. By April 1947 the city had built 709 'temporary' prefab bungalows and 1,000 permanent houses, by November another 1,000 had been completed, many using unconventional construction techniques, such as steel frames. Work began at Leigh Park in September 1947.

By May 1955 the council had built 9000 new homes since the end of the war. There were still housing problems, though, as the standard of what was acceptable had risen and the average number of people in each household was falling, meaning more homes were needed to house a given number of people. Demolition of the substandard buildings and rebuilding was seen as the only way forward, and over the next twenty years large areas of Portsmouth around the city centre were redeveloped, breaking up the established communities. Government subsidies and the newly perceived need to keep people on Portsea Island meant the building of high-rise blocks, such as Millgate House in St George's Square, occupied in 1964. The new homes were mostly much better than those they replaced, having bathrooms, for example, and much more green

space around them. There were some failures, however, such as Portsdown Park, begun in 1968. Portsdown Park was an extensive development on the slopes of Portsdown Hill, between the Queen Alexandra Hospital and the old A3. It consisted of a variety of building types, including high-rise blocks, built from designs chosen by an architectural competition. Because either the design or the construction was faulty, however, the buildings were unhealthily damp, the problems could not be remedied and the estate was demolished before it was twenty years old. By 1974 the council owned over 25,000 houses.

The problems that comprehensive redevelopment of an area caused led to a switch of policy towards refurbishment of existing buildings. In 1963 the council began giving housing improvement grants, and the first Comprehensive Improvement Area was declared in Stamshaw in 1971. There are now virtually no houses in Portsmouth which lack the basic amenities of hot water and an internal toilet. The house-building policy changed also. As barracks or naval bases were closed, most of the land was sold for privately-built housing, such as The Ridings, on the site of Hilsea Barracks, or Pembroke Park, where the Victoria Barracks stood. In the 1980s government controls on local authority spending brought council house building virtually to a halt, and housing associations such as The Portsmouth Housing Association took over as providers of 'social housing'.

The dominating factor in the city's history throughout the century has been its role as a naval base, with a large military garrison to protect the naval facilities. The First World War therefore had a dramatic effect on the lives of Portsmouth's people. They responded magnificently. Besides the many regular servicemen and territorial army soldiers, the city raised several battalions for the army. Some five thousand local men were killed, more than one in fifty of the city's inhabitants, while it is said that the Battle of Jutland, in which several Portsmouth ships were sunk, left 40 widows in one street. The names of the city's dead are listed on the war memorial beside the Guildhall; to stand and read them is a sobering experience. At home there was rationing and hundreds of women took on jobs which had been considered men's work, such as being a tram conductor. They even penetrated such bastions of male exclusiveness as the dockyard and gasworks. All but a few were laid off once the war ended. Several large local houses became temporary hospitals, such as Brankesmere in Kent Road, home of Sir John Brickwood (now used by Social Services). A Zeppelin's attempt to bomb the dockyard ended in failure, the bombs falling in the harbour. The dockyard refitted 1200 vessels during the war years, and completed the battleship *Royal Sovereign*.

The experience of Portsmouth during the Second World War was very different. Far fewer local servicemen (but more servicewomen) were killed, despite disasters such as the sinking of the *Royal Oak* and the *Hood*, both with enormous loss of life. Air raids, however, brought the war directly to Portsmouth's civilians, 930 of whom were killed and 1216 injured badly enough to be admitted to hospital. Physical destruction was widespread, 6625 properties were destroyed and 6549 seriously damaged. Most of these were homes, but the bombing destroyed also the shopping centres at Commercial Road, Kings Road and Palmerston Road, business premises as diverse as Hostler's sweet factory, Palmer's brush factory and the new Co-op store in Fratton, the Guildhall, the Eye and Ear Hospital, eight schools, many churches, several cinemas, the Hippodrome Theatre and Clarence Pier. The worst raids, with the heaviest casualties, were on the afternoon of 24 August 1940 and the nights of 10 January, 10 March and 27 April 1941. On 10 January the Germans dropped some 25,000 incendiary bombs as well as high-explosive bombs which broke the water mains and greatly hindered fire-fighting.

Total war led to the mobilisation of all sectors of Portsmouth's population. Thousands of children were evacuated as the war began and the schools were closed. A number reopened because many children returned during the 'Phoney War'. Several thousand Air-Raid Precaution workers were recruited, including a substantial and very-much needed reinforcement to the city's pitifully small police fire brigade in the shape of the Auxiliary Fire Service. Eleven local people won the George Medal, the second-highest award for courage given to civilians, for actions during the blitz. Once again there was rationing, but the diet of most people improved because the poorest could now afford to spend more on food as wartime wages rose and the shortage of fats, sugar and meat increased the proportion of bread and vegetables eaten by everyone else. Extra food could be bought at reasonable prices at one of the 'British Restaurants' run by the council. Local businesses switched to wartime production; one corset factory made waterproof cases for radios, for example, while White & Newton, the furniture manufacturer, made aircraft parts for Airspeed. Women once more took the jobs of absent men, especially after compulsory registration began in 1941. Not only did they become riveters, welders and electricians in the dockyard, but many worked for Airspeed, building aircraft, and two became Portsmouth's first female bus drivers. A few day nurseries were opened to help some women workers with childcare. Despite the hardships, the 'trekking' of many people to sleep outside the city during the worst of the bombing, the frequent air-raid warnings and the damage done by the enemy, wartime production in Portsmouth continued almost unabated.

The launch of the *Royal Sovereign* at the height of the First World War marked a pinnacle in the history of the dockyard. In the years before the war Britain entered into an armaments race with Germany. In Portsmouth dockyard the 'great factory' was built and the *Dreadnought* laid down in 1905. From her launch in 1906, after only a year's work, the yard built the first of each new class of dreadnought. The workforce grew in line with the tasks required of it. From employing nearly 8000 men in 1900, there were 15,000 in 1914 and a peak of 23,000 in 1917. When the war ended there were lay-offs, as after earlier wars, so by 1921 only 9,000 worked in the yard. With rearmament in the 1930s the dockyard workforce was expanded again, reaching some 14,000 by the outbreak of war, and around 25,000 before 1945. During the war the yard refitted and repaired over 2500 ships. The postwar rundown was slower than after 1918, but more complete. The last ship to be built in the yard, *HMS Andromeda*, was launched in 1967. Changes in military technology, especially missiles and air-power, together with a new political climate, have led to a run-down in the size of the Royal Navy, and Britain became over-supplied with dockyard facilities. By 1981 there were only 8000 people working in the dockyard. That year the Conservative government decided to reduce Portsmouth dockyard to the status of a naval base, shrinking its workforce to under three thousand. The rapid fitting out of the Falklands task force in 1982 was the yard's swansong, while the peace dividend created by the end of the Cold War has made the dockyard's resurgence still more unlikely. The Second World War, then, was a turning point in the yard's history as it was in the physical growth of the city.

The city's decline as a naval centre was matched by a loss of role as a military town. Portsmouth had had a garrison since the sixteenth century. In the nineteenth century its forts, intended to protect the dockyard, of course, not the townsfolk, had made it the best-defended town in Britain. There were thousands of soldiers in the town in 1901. Their barracks were prominent features of the townscape and the houses of the senior officers made a green enclave, now known as Ravelin Park. Fortifications dotted the southern shore of Portsea Island. The same technological developments that affected the navy made these defences superfluous. First Lumps Fort was sold, in the 1930s, then in the late 1950s and early '60s the remaining seafront bastions. They were mostly acquired by the city and a powerful heritage lobby persuaded the council to turn them into tourist attractions. Soldiers were no longer needed to man the defences and they were withdrawn. The Solent Garrison was formally disbanded in 1961. The barracks were closed and sold, the last being the Royal Marines Barracks at Eastney, sold off in the 1990s.

The city did benefit from this process, however, in that the run-down of defence establishments has released valuable land. New housing estates have appeared on all the former barrack sites except Point. The council was able to zone this newly available land for private housing rather than council estates, redressing the balance of postwar housing on Portsea Island. The Gunwharf, formerly the navy's torpedo and mine warfare training school, *HMS Vernon*, is the most recent example.

From the figures quoted above, it is clear that the dockyard was Portsmouth's major employer for much of the twentieth century. Such was the town's dependence on the dockyard that the layoffs led to severe unemployment locally during the early 1920s. There were still 9000 unemployed men and women in 1931. Soup kitchens had long been established by local churches, and there was a boot fund to provide shoes for poor children; now the council set up an unemployment committee to help ameliorate the problem. It ceased sitting in 1926, but the programme of public works it initiated to employ the workless, such as extending the esplanade to Eastney and building the Eastern Road, continued sporadically until the Second World War. The dockyard's dominance was reinforced by the Admiralty's long opposition to any expansion of the commercial port which might interfere with the naval base, and by the government's policy of undertaking as many tasks as possible within state-run establishments. The dockyard did not create much employment outside its walls, therefore, by sub-contracted work.

As a result, most of the other townspeople, at the start of the century, were employed in small-scale enterprises serving the needs of their neighbours. The wheelwrights, Hoads, whose equipment is now owned by Portsmouth Museums and Records Service, was one example; another was Treadgolds, an ironfactor and blacksmiths in Bishop Street, Portsea, whose premises are now a museum. There were some important exceptions, however. One of these was the Portsea Island Co-operative Society, founded in 1873, which in 1998 traded over 1000 square miles and had a turnover of nearly £200 million. In 1948 it opened the first self-service store in Britain, in Albert Road. Another was brewing. Portsmouth had 14 breweries in 1902, serving the thirsty soldiers and sailors and reaching out to a wider market. Mergers and problems reduced this to four by 1914, Brickwoods, Longs, Portsmouth United Breweries and Youngs. In the 1920s and '30s Brickwoods and United expanded beyond Portsmouth, acquiring breweries as far apart as Southampton and Brighton, while Longs became part of Brickwoods. Wartime bomb damage severely hampered the companies after the war, however, as shortage of cash and facilities undermined their attempts to compete in what was becoming a national market. Young's was absorbed by Friary Meux in 1959 and its Victory Brewery closed at once. Brickwoods and United merged in 1953; the joint company was sold to Whitbread in 1971, and brewing ceased at its Portsea site in 1983.

A local specialisation was the corset trade. Portsmouth had developed a corset-making industry of national significance during the nineteenth century. The town had a large pool of female labour, the wives of sailors and dockyardmen, seeking to eke out their husbands' scanty wages. The industry was ideally suited to a combination of factory work and home working, and it continued to flourish until after the Second World War. As late as 1971 there were eight fair-sized companies making corsetry and other women's underwear in Portsmouth including Berlei and the long-established local firms Leethems (whose brand name was 'Twilfit') and Weingartens. In 1998 there were only three small companies, including Vollers, founded about 1899 and still owned by the founder's family.

Two long-established Portsmouth firms became national names during the twentieth century. Timothy White opened an oil and drysaltery business in Portsea in 1848. He extended the range of goods on sale to include household items and medicines, becoming a pharmacist. Under the control of his son, Sir Woolmer White, the business expanded over the southern counties. In 1935 it merged with Taylors, a rival based in Leeds. By 1968, when it was bought by Boots, the company was the second largest chain of retail chemists in Britain, with 622 shops. The name was phased out in 1985. Gieves & Hawkes, the tailors, had its origins in a naval tailoring business founded by a Welshman, Melchisedek Meredith, in Old Portsmouth in 1785. Naval tailoring was a trade which long prospered in Portsmouth, and there are still several naval tailors operating in the city. By shrewd marketing as well as good tailoring James Watson Gieve expanded the business in the late-nineteenth and early-twentieth centuries so it catered for the majority of naval officers and had branches at all the major naval bases. The familiar Portsmouth shop on the Hard was opened in 1909. Expansion and a shift into new markets as the number of naval officers fell has taken the company's flagship shop to 1 Saville Row, London.

The citizens of Portsmouth had always been aware of the economic problems brought by relying on the dockyard, with its wartime expansions and postwar contractions. Ways were sought to broaden the town's commercial base. One was by promoting Southsea as a seaside resort. In the nineteenth century public subscriptions raised money for the creation of Clarence Esplanade, while Southsea Common was landscaped. The council leased the common from the government, laying out Ladies' Mile and Canoe Lake. Meanwhile, far-sighted entrepreneurs built Clarence and South Parade piers, and a string of hotels in Southsea. Some less-talented businessmen built the Southsea railway, a line from Fratton to Granada Road aimed at the tourist trade, which closed in 1914 because it generated so little traffic. The gentle curve of the track is clearly visible on maps, while on the ground twentieth-century houses set down among Victorian neighbours reveal its course. The station buildings became a garage and were demolished and redeveloped a few years ago.

This policy was continued by council and business community in the twentieth century, and many of the pictures reproduced in this book were taken for publicity purposes. A Southsea and Portsmouth Entertainment Committee was formed in 1905 to provide deckchairs, and so forth, for the resort. This committee was a private body because the council lacked the legal powers to take on the work. Most of its members were councillors, however. In 1919 the council appointed a Beach Committee and in 1920 it took over the

Entertainment Committee's assets. Already the council had stepped in when its owners had decided not to rebuild South Parade Pier after a fire. Now, in 1922, the borough went on to buy Southsea Common and provide new facilities for the resort: the bandstand, rock gardens, refreshment rooms, beach tents, children's pool and bowls and tennis courts. The creation of the municipal golf course at Great Salterns in 1926 and the later course at Crookhorn were both done with one eye on the tourist trade. Special open-sided 'runabout' buses were provided for the seafront in 1924. Entertainment was provided; not just the shows and dancing at South Parade Pier but, especially in the 1950s and '60s, beauty and fishing competitions. Private enterprise did its part, with boat trips on paddle steamers and power boats, dancehalls at the Savoy and Clarence Pier, the model village and the funfair. More recently has come the Sealife Centre and, as a joint council-private development, The Pyramids. Tourism was worth £228 million to the city in 1997 and supported 6700 jobs.

Hand-in-hand with the development of its facilities went campaigns to advertise the resort and liberalisation of social attitudes. In 1910 new by-laws were passed allowing men and women to bathe together; previously their bathing machines had to be stationed 50 yards (nearly 50m) apart. In 1933 local people voted to allow cinemas, theatres and sporting facilities to open on Sundays. To the scandal of the strict religious, the council then launched the 'Exit Mrs Grundy' campaign, advertising Southsea as 'the resort with no restrictions' on posters showing 'Mrs Grundy', a sour-looking old lady, hurrying to the station with a bag full of 'troubles'. A similar furore was raised in 1958, when a sultry-looking blonde in a bikini adorned the resort's posters, but instead of withdrawing the image the council launched a competition to find the girl who looked most like the one in the poster. Swimming costumes became more revealing as the century progressed. Until the 1940s men's costumes covered the chest, although many sunbathers rolled them down to the waist. Two-piece costumes for women were rare before the Second World War, although legs had been shortened to the top of the thigh. By the 1970s bikinis were often minuscule, while before the end of the '80s, however many men peeked, few people complained if a girl removed her bikini top altogether. The heyday of Southsea as a resort was in the 1930s and '50s. Cheap foreign holidays in the '60s undermined the attraction of the British seaside. The city's advertising strategy changed to

11

reflect this in the 1970s, laying increasing stress on Portsmouth's historic and naval heritage. This policy took concrete form in the creation of Southsea Castle and D-Day Museums and in support for the naval heritage attractions in the redundant, oldest part of the dockyard.

Besides the resort, the council tried to diversify the city's economy in other areas. One of the biggest steps was the creation of the municipal airport, opened in 1932. It not only allowed for air services from the city, but also created new opportunities for industry. The fledgling aircraft manufacturer Airspeed was attracted here from York in 1933. Its managing director was Neville Shute Norway, an engineer, who led the firm's development from a small business with 12 employees to a large organisation employing 1035 in 1938. Then he was ousted by the board, on good terms, for the company had yet to make a profit, and became a highly successful novelist. The company at last secured government contracts and its 'Oxford' became the principal training aircraft for bomber crews, while its 'Horsa' glider played a key role on D-Day, at Arnhem and the crossing of the Rhine. Airspeed was taken over by De Havilland in 1953 and the factory was closed in 1968. The main building still stands. Other successful businesses on the airfield site included Fireproof Tanks Ltd, which began as a subsidiary of Airspeed to make aircraft petrol tanks that sealed themselves if damaged, and Hants & Sussex Aviation, set up in 1946 to recondition aircraft engines and still flourishing.

The airfield operated with moderate success until the late 1960s. Channel Airways, flying to the Channel Islands, were established there in 1955. The company moved to Eastleigh, however, after it bought bigger aircraft and two of them crashed at Portsmouth in one day. The city's grass runways were too short in wet conditions for planes big enough to be commercially viable. An heroic attempt to set up an alternative service by JF Airlines was unable to revive the airport's finances, and it closed at the end of 1973.

As part of its new plan adopted in 1943, the council applied a policy of zoning activities: housing, shopping and industry. Before the war there was little to stop any business opening in a residential area, however noisome its activities, while there was danger that all the major roads would become lined with shops. After 1945 councils had new planning powers, and Portsmouth used them to create industrial estates. The first, at Fratton, opened in 1947. Companies setting up on the new estates included Johnson & Johnson and

Smith's Crisps. The result has been a gradual concentration of industry away from housing as companies closed or sold up and moved to better premises. When White & Newton's furniture factory in Dunbar Road closed in 1983, for example, its site was redeveloped for houses rather than sold to another manufacturer; the same is true of Vosper's shipyard, in Old Portsmouth. Much of this new industrial development has taken place on the east of Portsea Island, on sites such as that available after the closure of the gasworks at Hilsea and the airport. At the same time the council has continued to encourage large companies to set up in Portsmouth by offering cheap rents and good infrastructure. The most obvious results have been the location of IBM's British headquarters here in the early 1970s and the attraction of Zurich Insurance, while the defence-based company Marconi has established itself on the former airfield.

Effective transport is vital to a community's economic well-being. The railway had come to Portsmouth in 1847, run jointly by the London and South Western Railway and the London, Brighton and South Coast Railway. The two companies were merged in 1923 to form part of the Southern Railway, and this in turn was nationalised in 1948. In the 1990s the railways were privatised again; services from Portsmouth are now run by Connect South-Central and South-West Trains. Major changes have included the closure of the Southsea branch, the opening of halts at the racetrack at Paulsgrove and at Hilsea, the moving of the goods depot from Portsmouth and Southsea Station to Fratton in 1936, the electrification of the main line to London in 1937, and the replacement of the eight signal boxes by a single electrified box in 1968, which radically changed the working lives of signalmen.

No area of transport has been as important to Portsmouth in the twentieth century as its commercial docks. The Camber, around which the town had grown up, was used by coastal vessels for most of the century, bringing a variety of goods, in particular coal. Huge concrete coal bunkers stood on the southern side of East Street from the 1920s until the 1970s, with great cranes for unloading colliers at the adjacent jetty. The power station had a dock, on the site of the graving dock, for landing its fuel, linked to the main site by a high-level conveyor. Today the harbour is little used other than by the port's fleet of inshore fishing boats, now with engines in contrast to the sailing boats usual before 1939. Facilities for larger vessels were created at Flathouse in the 1860s, and this wharf was expanded to form the Albert Johnson Quay, opened in 1968. Dredging of this part of the harbour and the building of refrigerated warehouses allowed Portsmouth to become the largest fruit importing port in Britain by 1995, much visited by banana boats. In the 1970s facilities for large roll-on, roll-off ferries were created nearby, and the port quickly captured Southampton's ferry trade. In 1997 3,282,604 passengers passed through the ferry port, and it has become an important part of the city economy. Fortunately for the city the port facilities were too small to be included in the nationalisation of British ports in 1969.

Within the city, public transport has passed from private ownership to municipal control and back again. In 1901 the council bought the tramway system, by compulsory purchase, and at once began to electrify the system. The first electric trams ran that September; the last horse-drawn trams in 1903. Portsmouth Corporation Tramway's trams ran to Cosham. From 1903 the Portsdown & Horndean Light Railway ran trams from there to Horndean, thereby easing the development of the communities along the line of the A3. By 1930 the city's trams were wearing out and competition from the more modern Southdown buses meant they were operating at an increasing loss. In 1934 it was decided to replace them with electric trolleybuses, and the last tram ran in 1936. Meanwhile Southdown had bought and in 1935 closed the P&HLR. The trolleybuses could pick up passengers from the side of the road, unlike trams, and were very popular. By the 1960s, however, this system, too, needed expensive refurbishment, while the rising numbers of private cars was reducing the number of passengers. The last trolleybus ran in 1963. One-man operation of motor buses had been carried out occasionally since the 1920s, and to reduce costs in the face of ever-larger numbers of cars, all Portsmouth's buses became one-man operated in 1980. The government felt that such measures could not alone solve the problem of falling passenger numbers and higher subsidies, and deregulated the bus industry. In 1986 the City of Portsmouth Passenger Transport Department became a private company, Portsmouth City Transport Ltd. PCT quickly became Portsmouth City Bus, then in 1989 part of Stagecoach, along with Southdown. With too great a monopoly, Stagecoach was obliged by the government to sell City Bus, which was taken over by Red and Blue Admiral. A radical new approach was adopted and the traditional double-deckers were almost all replaced by short-wheelbase, minibus-like single-deckers. Within a few years the company was sold to Provincial, the successor of the company from which the council had bought the tramway at the start of the century.

At the beginning of the twentieth century, religious life in Portsmouth was in a healthy state. Kelly's directory for 1901 lists 91 churches, chapels and mission rooms holding regular services, and a synagogue. St Mary's church in particular was the centre of a flourishing parish community, and under successive vicars Cosmo Lang, Bernard Wilson and Cyril Garbett, was a model of parish organisation. The Six [Portsmouth] Churches Fund, launched in 1913, paid for more badly-needed and imposing buildings, including St Cuthbert's and St Alban's, Copnor, and St John's, Rudmore. In 1927 the city became the seat of a new Anglican diocese; Neville Lovett was its first bishop. St Thomas's church was chosen as cathedral over St Mary's because of its historical associations and fine medieval chancel, and perhaps to avoid disrupting St Mary's parish life. In 1935 work began on enlarging the building, but construction was halted by the war. Fund-raising in the 1960s to complete it to striking new designs by Pier Nervi and Paul Paget failed to reach the necessary target; a scheme more in keeping with the existing structure was completed in 1992. Five Anglican and several nonconformist churches were not rebuilt after the destruction of the Second World War. Instead new buildings, such as St Michael's, Paulsgrove, and Paulsgrove Baptist church, were erected on the new estates. They differed strikingly from pre-war churches, being designed more to meet the needs of worship and the congregation than to impress. The churches played a big role in the social lives of those living in Paulsgrove and Leigh Park, but gradually religion has become less central in Portsmouth people's lives. The 1998 Yellow Pages listed only 25 places of worship in Portsmouth. Nevertheless, in 1985 2.3 per cent of the population of the Anglican Diocese of Portsmouth still went to church on Sundays, while ethnic groups coming to Portsmouth in recent years have brought new religions with them. Portsmouth's Islamic community has grown sufficiently to need a second mosque.

Charity based on religious ethics was certainly one motive that Portsmouth people had for supporting their local hospitals. Before the creation of the NHS, all but a few had to pay for their medical care. The town had six civil hospitals. The oldest was the Royal Portsmouth Hospital, founded in 1847, which stood just behind Commercial Road, where Sainsbury's is today. It was an independent institution, supported by donations and fund-raising. The war memorial fund of 1919 paid for one extension. Patients were expected to contribute to the cost of their treatment; an early form of medical insurance for the working classes was the Dockyard All-in Scheme, launched in 1926 and later extended to workers elsewhere in the city, by which a payment of 2d a week covered their and their family's hospital care. By the 1970s many of its buildings were very old, while there was no room to expand, or for car parking. In 1978 it was closed, most of its facilities having been transferred to the Queen Alexandra. The other independent hospital was the Portsmouth & South Hants Eye & Ear Infirmary, opened in Pembroke Road in 1884, which had 48 beds by 1914. This hospital was destroyed by bombing in 1941, and after several moves in 1944 was settled in the former Convent of the Holy Cross, Grove Road North. During the 1960s its functions were gradually transferred to the QA, and it closed in 1969. The other hospitals were both supported from public funds. St Mary's Hospital began as the infirmary wing of the workhouse, and not until 1930 was it thrown open to the ratepayers as a whole. By the 1960s St Mary's had a specialism in maternity and baby care. There, in 1968, for the first time a complete blood change was carried out on a baby before birth. Across the road from it was the Infectious Diseases Hospital, opened in 1883 when isolation and rest were almost the only treatment for a number of serious illnesses. Even in the 1930s diphtheria patients spent weeks or months on their backs, simply resting. By 1922 it had 265 beds and treated a thousand patients a year; a large extension was opened in 1938. As medical science developed isolation wards were no longer needed. The hospital was amalgamated with St Mary's in 1968, and its buildings have recently been demolished. Linked to the IDH were the Locks Hospital for Smallpox, and the Langstone Hospital for the treatment of tuberculosis, which replaced it in 1911. As treatment of TB improved immediately after the Second World War and better living standards made the disease rarer, this hospital, too, closed. Two other hospitals were supported by local ratepayers. St James's opened in 1879 as the Borough of Portsmouth Lunatic Asylum. Its running costs were offset by its farm, where patients worked as a form of occupational therapy, that operated until 1965. A full-time occupational therapist was first employed only in 1964, a sign of the dramatically changing conditions for the mentally ill. The other was a small maternity hospital, opened in 1920 in Elm Grove and in 1927 transferred to Trafalgar Place. It closed in 1938. The Queen Alexandra began as a military hospital. In 1941 it admitted its first civilian patients; by 1951 all but 100 of

its beds had been taken over by the NHS. In the last fifty years the QA has become the biggest hospital in south-east Hampshire as a variety of functions have been centralised there including accident and emergency work. By 1988 it had over 1000 staff.

The foundations of the modern educational system in Portsmouth were laid by the school boards, the first of which was elected in 1871. In 1903, when the School Board handed over to the new Local Education Authority, the town had 36 primary schools and a secondary school for boys, as well as the long-established Portsmouth Grammar School and a number of private schools. The development of local schools since then has followed the national pattern. The school leaving age was raised to fourteen in 1918, to fifteen in 1944 and sixteen in 1973. More secondary schools were provided: there were four council-run secondary schools, two for boys and two for girls, in 1937. Now there are eleven. After the Second World War a system of 'modern', 'technical' and 'grammar' secondary schools was introduced, with selection based on the 11 Plus. Comprehensive schools replaced this system in 1975, rather later than elsewhere. There are now 66 state schools in the city, together with a few grant-maintained and private schools. In recent years the number of nursery schools has also risen, partly as a result of financial support for them by the government. At the other end of the spectrum, in 1900 the borough already had tertiary education at its Technical Institute, founded in 1894. This became the Municipal College, and associated with it and sharing its new building was the School of Art. From 1907 the borough also ran a training college for female teachers, for which buildings were provided at Milton in the late 1930s. Highbury Technical College was created in 1962 to take over the college's non-advanced courses, and the main institution became a polytechnic in 1969. In 1992 it finally became a university, and now has over 8000 students.

In core areas of the city's life, then, Portsmouth has been transformed over the last century. Although it is now scarcely bigger than it was in 1900, its population is better housed, wealthier, more thoroughly educated and healthier to an older age. It has survived the traumas of two major wars and the decline of the dockyard, the staple of its economy a hundred years ago. It has diversified that economy, strengthening it against possible future risks. As the piles for the Millennium Tower are sunk, it stands in a good position to handle the challenges of the twenty-first century – continued economic change, technological revolution, the motor car, rising sea levels, or whatever they may be.

1900 – 1909

Portsmouth Town Hall. Opened on 9 August 1890 by TRH The Prince and Princess of Wales, this splendid new building replaced the earlier Town Hall constructed in the High Street in 1837. It was built of Portland stone and cost £145,000. This photograph was taken on the occasion of the visit of the French Northern Squadron to Portsmouth in August 1905. (1607A/1)

The Council Chamber in the new Town Hall. The interior of the Town Hall, known as the Guildhall after 1926, when Portsmouth became a city, was destroyed by fire on the night of 10-11 January 1941.

(407A/4/6)

Commercial Road sweeps across the foreground in this photograph of the area known better today as Guildhall Square. Russell Street extends south towards Hyde Park Road. The statue of Queen Victoria, unveiled in July 1903, can be seen in the middle ground.

(407A/4/10)

The New Theatre Royal, as we know it today, was opened on 6 August 1900. It was designed by Frank Matcham, the most experienced architect on theatre design in the country. The original New Theatre Royal opened on this site in 1856 and was subjected to a number of interior and exterior alterations between 1868 and 1884. The 1900 rebuild produced a stage which was one of the largest in the country, capable of taking the most elaborate scenery and with a run-in adequate for galloping horses! The Hippodrome, a music hall, on the opposite side of the road, opened in 1907. It was destroyed in the big blitz of 10-11 January 1941.   (PCM)

The Hippodrome.   (941A/11/8ph)

Between 1902 and 1904 St Thomas's church, Portsmouth's ancient parish church, was extensively restored and, subsequently, re-ordered. Centuries of intra-mural interments had seriously undermined foundations and structure and by 1902 posed a major public health risk. The decayed coffins and human remains were gathered together and sealed in large vaults beneath nave and chancel. The re-opening ceremony took place on 8 November 1904 in the presence of HRH Princess Henry of Battenburg, Queen Victoria's youngest daughter, Princess Beatrice.

(548A/23/13 & 1102/1980C)

The foundation stone of the Roman Catholic Cathedral of St John the Evangelist in Edinburgh Road was laid on 9 December 1881. It was opened on 10 October 1882. Additions were carried out by J. S. Hanson in 1886 and 1892. The building was completed finally in 1906 with a west end and porch by Canon A. J. C. Scoles. Bishop's House, on the right in the lower picture, was destroyed in the Second World War. (407A/4)

Portsmouth from the Gosport side of the harbour. The floating bridge is in the middle of the photograph. Incorporated in 1838, it began running in 1840. *HMS Victory* is moored nearest the shore. (681A/1/2)

The corporation acquired in 1903 the house in which Charles Dickens was born on 7 February 1812. It opened as the Dickens Museum on 22 July 1904. (1066/1980K)

On 10 February 1906, HM King Edward VII launched *HMS Dreadnought* from its building slip in the Dockyard. She marked a new epoch in battleship construction. All records were beaten in her construction. She was the most powerful battleship in the world. She was launched after only five months on the stocks and commissioned just one year after the laying of her first keel plates. The lower photograph shows the laying of the keel plates, September 1905.

(946A/4ph & 1083A/58)

A view of the dockyard c.1908 with, in the foreground, the Gosport ferries and the railway line opened 1876, constructed as part of the harbour extension across the foreshore of Watering Island. The jetty here was constructed in 1860 and was especially suitable for troopships.

(814A/2)

March Past! Local schoolchildren celebrating in their playground the visit of the French fleet to Portsmouth in 1905.

(1437A/1/3/2)

Japanese battleships visited Portsmouth in 1906 and 1907. The visiting sailors were taken on a trip into the local countryside on the newly-constructed (1903) Portsdown and Horndean Light Railway. The building of this tramway was a key factor in the development of the Portsmouth-Horndean corridor.

(DR/P/78)

The Carnegie Library opened on 12 September 1906. The Scottish-born Pittsburg millionaire, Andrew Carnegie, gave £4,500 towards the cost on condition the town gave a site and maintained the library. It was designed free of charge by local architects Rake and Cogswell.

(PCM)

The Municipal College, behind the Town Hall, was opened in September 1908 by the Mayor, Mr F G Foster. The Mayor, a widower, was accompanied by his small daughter, Doris, aged $5^1/_2$ who had been installed as his Mayoress. As a former Chairman of the Education Committee, the Mayor had played a key role in developing the College, new buildings to rehouse the Technical Institute in Arundel Street, which were erected at the hitherto unheard-of cost for an educational institution of £120,000. (681A/3/3/7)

The Public Library was located on the ground floor of the new building. It remained there until 1976.

(407A/4/8)

The laying of the foundation stone of the Portsmouth Workhouse Infirmary Extension Block, 1908. The new provision included a maternity block and four extra wards. The hospital is better known today as St Mary's Hospital.

(H/73/86)

Begun in 1904, occupied in 19 March 1908, and known today as Queen Alexandra Hospital, this former military hospital now provides hospital services for much of south-east Hants with its sister-hospital, St Mary's, the former Poor Law Infirmary.

(1064/1980A)

South Parade Pier was destroyed by fire on 19 July 1904. The structure remained derelict for some time before the corporation resolved to acquire it and rebuild it on a grander scale.

(190/1981C)

The new South Parade Pier is under construction here on 7 May 1908. It opened later in the year. For some years it failed to make a great deal of money but later became one of the city's most famous attractions. It was destroyed by fire in its turn in 1974.

(DA/2/B/534)

Roller skating on South Parade Pier, c.1908. (167A/3)

Bathing machines on Southsea Beach c.1907. (PCM)

Easter Monday 1903. Bank holiday crowds wait for train to pass at the level crossing at Cosham. (658/1964)

Portsmouth welcomes back its Olympic champion, the cyclist C. B. Kingsbury, who won two gold medals at the 1908 Olympic Games held that year in London. (522/70)

Church Parade. Sunday morning after church on the Ladies' Mile, Southsea, c.1909. (17A/3/17)

Hoad and Sons, coachbuilders, c.1900. The firm was established in 1799 at Kingston Crescent, Portsmouth. After a fire in 1913 the business moved to Basin Street, where it continued at a reduced level until the 1980s. (1433A/10/2)

An unknown brickworks, possibly in the Stamshaw area, c.1900-5. Most of Portsmouth's houses were built of bricks manufactured from brick-earth dug alongside the building site. (1499A/31)

Interior of printers, Coasby and Co, before the First World War. (1143A/8/3/2)

1910 – 1919

Broad Street, about 1910. The vehicles on the left are queuing to board the Portsmouth-Gosport floating bridge, just around the corner. (772/1980)

Sir Charles Douglas receiving the salute of the guard of honour when he arrived at Portsmouth and Southsea Station to inspect the garrison, 15 March 1910. Sir Charles, who had joined the army in 1869, had just been promoted general. (1083A/42)

In March 1910 a small Russian squadron arrived at Spithead for a visit of several days. At the same time the Japanese warship *Ikoma* also came to Portsmouth and its crew were entertained by the borough to a banquet. The photographer wrote that this photo shows 'the extraordinary scene' of a Russian and a Japanese sailor shaking hands while being cheered by all nationalities at the mayor's garden party. Those two nations had been at war only five years before. (1083A/132)

'The old and the new, a striking contrast.' *HMS Nelson*, having been sold out of service on 12 July 1910, is shown lying near *HMS Neptune*, whose career was just beginning. *Nelson* was a protected cruiser, lightly armoured and using sails as well as engines, laid down in 1876. *Neptune* was a dreadnought battleship of 19,900 tons, laid down in Portsmouth dockyard in 1909 and commissioned in January 1911. (1083A/55)

The Beneficial School football team, 1910-11. The Beneficial School drew its pupils from one of Portsmouth's least prosperous communities, where many parents could not afford to buy their children shoes. Someone has provided these boys with boots and a strip. (536A/20/4/2b)

Sailors at play, snowballing each other along St James's Road, Southsea. (1083A/125)

The roadway under the railway across Commercial Road frequently flooded, especially after the surface was lowered to give enough headroom for trams to pass under the bridge. August, 1911. (494A/35ph)

The fire at the Royal Beach Hotel, 1911. 'The fire at its height, as seen from the rear of the hotel, sightseers clambering up on prominent places to get a good view.' The damage was confined to the upper part of the hotel and no-one was hurt.

(1083A/10)

The view from the Gosport pontoon looking towards Portsmouth dockyard, showing *HMS Victory* still afloat. The Semaphore Tower was burnt down in 1913, so the photograph was taken before then. The tower was reopened in 1930.

(681A/1/1)

The royal train leaving South Railway Jetty in the dockyard, probably after collecting Their Majesties on their return from India in 1912. The naval guard-of-honour is seen presenting arms, wearing their distinctive 'sennet' hats.

(1083A/49)

In 1912 the peal of eight bells in St Thomas' church tower were recast as part of the restoration of the structure. Each bell was paid for by a different section of the community, including the children of the town, Portsmouth's doctors, its lawyers, the army and the navy. (161A/3/1ph)

Man and motorcycle, about 1915. Motorcycles became a popular form of transport in this decade among the young, adventurous and technically-minded. There were dozens of British manufacturers, including the Osborne Engineering Co., founded in Gosport in 1919. (858a/3/74)

Whilst the *Prospector* was being warped out of Portsmouth Harbour the very strong tide that runs at Point caught the vessel and swept her on to the beach. She came to rest right across the floating bridge chains, making it impossible for vehicles to be taken across the harbour. (1083A/52)

W. J. Baily winning the one mile match against Leon Meredith at the Portsmouth Cycling Tournament at Alexandra Park shortly before the First World War. Judging by the crowds, cycle racing was as popular then as 'Le Tour' was when it came to Portsmouth in 1994.   (1083A/138)

'Queen Pansy, Portsmouth's May Queen, received a splendid ovation in the May Day procession. She is seen at the town hall with her maids of honour in a gorgeous white motor car, preparing to lead the procession, which was a mile long.' The photo is undated, but the town's May Day processions became a major public event in the years before the Great War.   (1083A/4)

How the other half lived! A delightful but very posed photo of two young girls, possibly of the Rands family. The Rands were jewellers in Palmerston Road, who ran a business under the name of Jackson (its earlier owner). The teddy bear with the long arms is probably German. Is the bird in the cage real or an automaton? Children from poor families had few toys, often homemade and very unlike these expensive playthings. (941A/10/38)

'William Clare, the alleged spy, making copious notes as the evidence for the prosecution proceeds.' Clare was a dentist with a surgery in Portsea. He was also a pimp, living off the immoral earnings of his wife, a prostitute serving Portsmouth's soldiers and sailors. In 1913 he was caught with a copy of the annual report about the development of torpedoes at *HMS Vernon*, for which Germany had offered him £300. He was sentenced to five years penal servitude. (1083A/24)

Torpedo-boat destroyers, about 1914. 'A striking photograph showing a flotilla of torpedo-boat destroyers steaming full speed up Portsmouth Harbour with torpedo tubes ready for use, giving an idea of how disastrous it would be to warships within the harbour should torpedo boats manage to evade the defences and pass the booms.' A barrier of concrete blocks, still visible, was put in the sea off Eastney to prevent such attacks on Spithead.

(1083A/73)

Winnie, the pet monkey of the Portsmouth-based destroyer, *Velox*, underwent an operation for an abcess on the head. The animal was an out-patient for ten days, being brought back each day to the hospital by his 'bluejacket' keeper. The sailor is seen dressing Winnie after his bath. The *Velox* was sunk by a mine near the Nab in 1915.

(1083A/124)

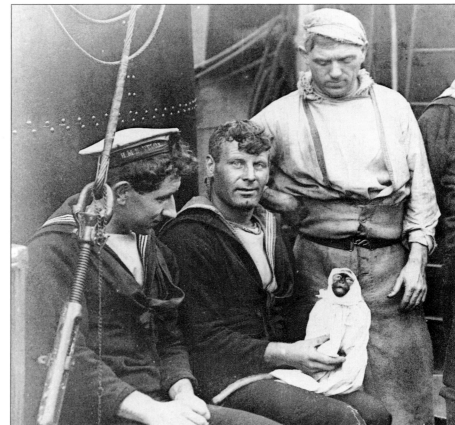

This photograph of territorial soldiers in camp is believed to have been taken in the local area, perhaps Lovedean. During the First World War Hampshire territorial units served in France, Belgium, Gallipoli, Italy, Persia, Mesopotamia, Salonika, Egypt, Palestine, Aden, India and Siberia. (1306A/1/24)

A beautifully-posed studio portrait of 12 women who worked in the Block Mills in the dockyard during the First World War. The caps were worn at all times to prevent hair getting caught in machinery. The triangular badges were marked 'On war service'. (1351A/1/1)

These women were helping the war effort by working at the gasworks. Note the older men in the centre of the photo, left to supervise whilst the young men went off to war. During the First World War many jobs usually done by men were filled by women. When the men returned from the forces the women were discharged.

(45A/11/3)

A comfort fund was set up by female volunteers to pay for food parcels to be sent to British prisoners-of-war. The first 180, containing such things as Oxo cubes, Huntley & Palmer biscuits and tinned meat, were despatched in 1916. Even though there were serious food shortages, and rationing, during 1917 and 1918 the volunteers managed to send nearly 17,000 parcels.

(687A/1/3)

A Salvation Army Band playing at a garden party at Wymering Manor in July 1916. This party was arranged by Muriel Cambie, a local war-worker, to entertain some 1600 widows, children and parents of servicemen killed during the war. They were given plates decorated with the flags of the allied nations and a patriotic and sentimental verse. Some 5,000 Portsmouth men had been killed by 1918. (523/1987)

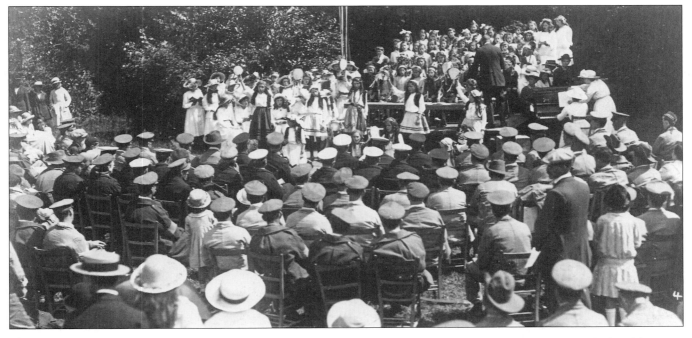

The Lake Road Band of Hope Choir entertaining wounded soldiers at Horndean at an event organised by Post Office staff, July 1918. These men are wearing red and blue army hospital uniforms. Two city schools and a number of private houses served as temporary hospitals, supplementing the Queen Alexandra military hospital. (605/1992c)

War Bond appeal, probably during 'Tank Week', December 1917. War bonds were a loan to the government to pay for the resources to continue the war. Portsmouth raised £4,027,000 in less than two years, £160,000 during Tank Week alone. Arguably, tanks played a more valuable role as propaganda instruments than on the battlefield. (1088A/2/60)

Portsmouth's first 10 motor buses, shown here arriving outside the town hall in July 1919, were J-type Thornycrofts, engineered in Basingstoke and with bodies made by Wadham Bros of Waterlooville. They were in service for about a decade, but the solid tyres, stiff suspension and rough road surfaces so damaged their body-work that about 1926 they were refitted with secondhand bodies from older London buses. One has been preserved by Portsmouth Museums and Records Service. (DR/P/79)

A carnival float advertising the uses of gas, photographed outside the Municipal College about 1919.

(45A/11/7)

One of Portsmouth Borough Police Force's first three policewomen, recruited in 1919. The experiment was not considered a success, and when the force was reduced from 308 to 290 in 1922 the remaining two were asked to resign. Policewomen were not appointed again until 1948. (1107/1980)

'Jack and Joey discuss the pay rise.' In 1919, under pressure from the navy, the Treasury allowed substantial increases to the pay of all ranks. An able seaman's pay went up from 1s 8d to 4s a day, while a captain's pay doubled. The officers' salaries were linked to the cost of living, however, while the wages of other ranks were not, which stored up trouble for the future.

(1083A/122)

An outing to Portchester Castle by one of Portsmouth's camera clubs, 1919. (PCM)

A dinner given in the town hall for the members of the 6th Battalion of the Hampshire Regiment on their return to England in 1919. (354A/1/3/1)

1920 – 1929

Entrance to a house, 'The Vale' in Clarendon Road, Southsea, 1920.   (PCM)

Maypole dancing at Highland Road School, about 1920. (1222A/2)

A Colyer and Company lorry, towing a tram body from Cosham railway station to the tram depot in North End. Twelve double-deck, covered-top tram bodies were delivered to Portsmouth between October 1920 and November 1926. Colyer and Co. were forced to close later in the 1920s, a victim of the Depression. (613/1992F)

Cities all over the country sought ways to remember the young men who had been killed in the First World War. The Duke of Connaught unveiled Portsmouth's War Memorial on 19 October 1921, watched by a crowd of at least 30,000.

(621/1992X)

The mayor, Mr Albert Edward Porter, greeted by Neptune and his attendants on Southsea Common at the town's first carnival, 1922. The event raised £8000 which was given to the Royal Portsmouth Hospital.

(1088A/2/65)

The War Memorial was officially handed over to Portsmouth on Easter Sunday 1922. On 28 July of that year, George V and Queen Mary paid a surprise visit to the city and inspected the new memorial.

(1088A/2/16)

Beauty contest for young children in Victoria Park, 1922, judged by the mayor, Albert Edward Porter.

(1088A/2/65)

A group of French children from areas of France devastated by the war, on the Town Hall steps with Alderman A. E. Porter, c.1922. (1088A/2/61)

The arches through Hilsea Lines under demolition in 1922/3. Hilsea Lines were erected in 1861, but large chunks were removed to improve access to the island. (783/1980E)

Opening of the Western Road to Paulsgrove on 26 October 1922. Built across the marshes, this was one of several road building schemes carried out in the 1920s that provided work for many of the unemployed. (1088A/2/26)

Sir Sydney and Lady Fremantle on the air railway, probably at a fête held for charity at Southsea Castle in 1923 or 1924. (998A/1/76)

'Santa Claus' distribution, Christmas 1923. The 1920s were a time of real hardship for many families in the city. The Evening News ran a Goodwill Fund to help those most in need. In 1921 the council voted £25,000 relief for the unemployed during the winter and in 1926 a group of local ladies collected enough money from friends to deliver presents to 3000 homes.

(998A/1/16)

Inauguration of the new Portsmouth District of the English Bowling Association, Saturday, 17 May 1924.

(998A/1/33)

Crowds on Southsea beach watch the fleet review in 1924. Only 10 battle-ships were present, in marked contrast to the review of 1914, which saw 55. A new class of ship made its first review appearance, the minesweeper. In the background, the naval war memorial takes shape in a cage of scaffolding.

(649/1945Q)

Unveiling of the Portsmouth Naval War Memorial by the Duke of York, 15 October 1924. The memorial was erected by the Imperial War Graves Commission to commemorate the 9700 officers and men of the Portsmouth Division who lost their lives in the war but had no known burial place.

(998A/1/50)

Mr Tom Foot and his wife, Lily, outside their home, Highgrove Farm, Hilsea, c.1925. (527/1993a)

McCreary's Stores, 34 Marmion Road, Christmas 1926. (299/1980)

HMS Furious, an early aircraft carrier, at Navy Days, probably in 1927. Then as now, the carriers always drew large crowds. In the background can be seen the steelwork for the reconstruction of the Semaphore Tower, which had burned down in 1913.   (194A/3/29)

Procession in Portsmouth High Street for the enthronement of the city's first bishop, the Venerable Ernest Neville Lovett, on 6 October 1927. The 1920s saw two important changes in status for Portsmouth: the declaration of Portsmouth as a cathedral town on 15 July 1924 following the division of the diocese of Winchester and the granting of city status on 21 April 1926.

(Courtesy of *The News*, CHU3/6B/4)

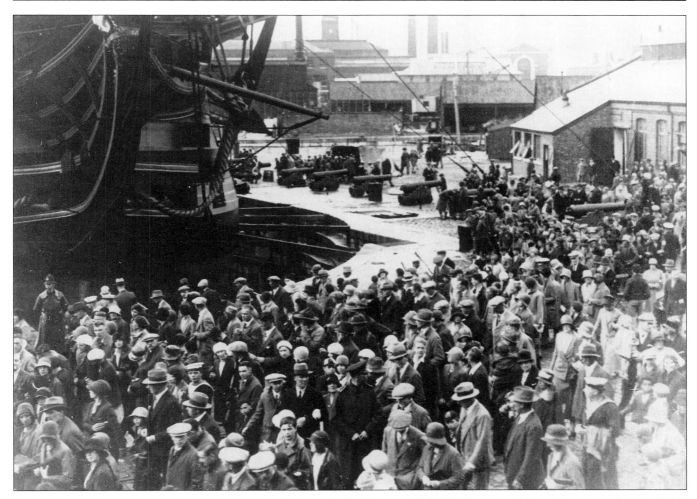

Crowds around the bows of *HMS Victory* at Navy Days, probably 1928. *Victory* was dry docked in 1922 after an appeal by the Society for Nautical Research to save her for the nation. Restoration work, to return her to her Trafalgar state, began immediately and was officially completed in 1928; George V visited her to mark the occasion. She was an instant success with the people at Navy Days and work continues today to restore her more accurately, in preparation for the bicentenary of the Battle of Trafalgar in 2005.

(657/1945P)

Iris Voss, aged 6, outside her home in Hereford Street, Landport, 1929. She remembers playing in the street, including traditional games of hopscotch and whip and top. She is shown with her new pram, probably on her birthday.

(509/1993)

Slum clearance, White's Row, Portsea, about 1929. In the early years of the century, Portsea already had a reputation as an area of slums, rife with vice and disease, but little was done until after the First World War. The issue was brought to a head by the murder of Mary Pelham, a prostitute, in Blossom Alley. The newspapers focused public attention on the appalling conditions and in 1929 a huge rehousing scheme started in Portsea. (477A/4/59)

Garden party at Wymering Manor in the 1920s, possibly held for war widows. (652/1945N)

The bandstand and terraces, Southsea Common, probably in the late 1920s. In December 1922 the town council decided to purchase Southsea Common from the War Office rather than continue to pay rent, and paid £45,000 for the 171 acres. A further £60,000 was spent on providing gardens and facilities for the common, including the bandstand, which proved very popular.

(657/1945A)

A charabanc outing for a picnic. Sadly the location shown in this photograph is unknown.

(621/1992N)

A men's day trip to the Meon Valley, leaving from outside the King and Queen, possibly Cosham.   (681A/1/3)

A fashion show of evening wear c.1925. Women's fashion in the 1920s saw a wide variation in dress lengths, but the most important feature was to look as 'boyish' as possible, with straight dresses disguising the feminine figure.

(496A/1/244)

Palmerston Road, c.1928, with Wendover & Co. Ltd on the left and Handleys in the distance. George Wendover began business as a cabinet maker and upholsterer at 55 and 56 Hanover Street, Portsea, in about 1855; his son had joined him by 1859. The business continued to grow and by 1890 it had moved to Palmerston Road, where it was a well-known firm until 1976, even surviving the upheaval of the Second World War.   (PCM)

1930 – 1939

North End, about 1930. The large house standing in its own grounds halfway between Laburnum Road and Stubbington Avenue was called Woodcrofts. It was home to Alderman Charles Dye. The alderman died in September 1932 during his honeymoon, two days after marrying his third, much younger, wife. His widow sold the house to a cinema chain and in 1937 the Odeon North End opened on the site. (PCM)

Regent Picture Theatre, c. 1938. The Regent, the large circular building in the bottom right of the aerial photograph of North End, opened its doors on 31 March 1923. Cinema-going was an extremely popular pastime and by the outbreak of the Second World War there were 27 cinemas in Portsmouth, capable of seating 32,014 people, 1908 of whom were accommodated at the Regent. (1629A/1/4)

The view across Canoe Lake c. 1930. The large white building across the lake is Cumberland House, which was purchased by the city in 1930 as the third of its museums. Local residents were relieved when the city acquired the house as there had been rumours that the site was going to become a petrol filling station which would have meant '... cars, lock-ups and traffic obstruction at a most important corner and would have become an intolerable nuisance'.

(1016/1973)

Miss Batchelor's class, Bramble Road Infants, 1931. When this school opened in 1887 the desks were arranged in tiers. The dark-painted area sloping down the wall bears witness to this layout. By the time this photo was taken the room had been levelled, leaving the windows set high in the wall - no glimpses of the outside world to distract these pupils! Chalk and boards were still in use, and hanging beside each desk is a bag in which the children kept their chalk, duster, and items such as knitting.

(H/1999/73)

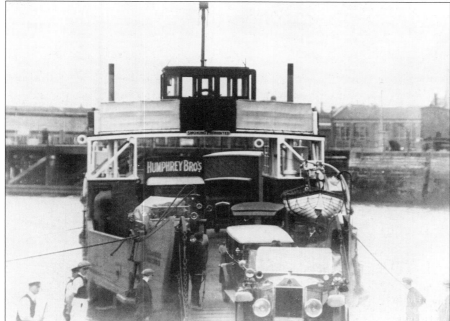

A ward in the Royal Portsmouth Hospital, Christmas 1931. The Royal stood in Commercial Road, where Sainsbury's is today.   (PCM)

Car ferry to the Isle of Wight, c. 1930. The first roll-on-roll-off ferry on the Portsmouth to Fishbourne route was introduced by the Southern Railway in 1927. This picture shows the ferry *Fishbourne* in 1930 as the cars disembark at Point at the end of Broad Street.   (1712A/2/1/57)

Before the opening of the city airport, land at Great Salterns was used as a private aerodrome by the local flying club. Amongst its many visitors were the famous aviator Amy Johnson and her husband, Jim Mollison, photographed here about 1930. Johnson was also seen in Portsmouth in the summer of 1930 as a guest of the Lord Mayor during a fortnight of civic festivities to celebrate the adoption of the city's motto 'Heaven's Light our Guide' (registered 1929). She landed her plane *Jason* at Alexandra Park prior to joining the Lord Mayor at the Guildhall.   (166A)

Portsmouth Municipal Airport opened on 2 July 1932. In the early days of aviation the spectacle of aeroplanes taking off and landing was a source of great interest and 'plane spotting' at Portsmouth aerodrome became a popular spectator sport. With cafe facilities capable of providing refreshment for over 100 people and aerial tours around the Isle of Wight available for a mere 5s (25p) per head, a good day out could be had by all. *(257/1989)*

The council created the airfield in order to attract industry. One of the new firms was Airspeed. Here a wooden biplane is under construction about 1933, but the company went on to produce revolutionary designs and pioneered the retractable undercarriage. Its managing director was Neville Shute Norway, who later became a successful popular novelist.

(597/1992)

The last tram, 10 November 1936. Seen here at journey's end at the Eastney depot, Car No. 106 was the last tram to run in Portsmouth. Just thirty-five years after its introduction the electric tram system had become obsolete. It was superseded by the popular trolleybus. (576A/1)

A trolleybus in London Road, North End, 1939. 'In view of the increasing loss upon the trams and the increasing profit on the buses', Mr Ben Hall, General Manager of Portsmouth Corporation Tramways, recommended in June 1934 that the council should 'scrap the trams entirely and as soon as possible substitute the trolleybus'. This proposal was taken up and in that same year the first electric trolleybus was put into service in Portsmouth.

(DR/P/48)

Park's was a haulage contractor which specialised in large or heavy loads. In this picture of about 1937 a steam tractor is pulling a low loader laden with a large-calibre coastal defence gun, which has been removed from its battery on the Isle of Wight. Behind is a Leyland lorry driven by Mr Cyril Stares that provided extra power on hills.

(H/133/97)

Hostlers Wholesale Confectioners, 367 Commercial Road. Alfred Hostler Ltd manufactured its 'pure boiled sweets' in Cosham Street, Landport, from the mid-1920s until 1941, when the factory was destroyed in the Blitz. The company distributed its goods from this site in Commercial Road until 1970 when the building was demolished to make way for the Church Street roundabout (by the ABC cinema). (241/1995)

Is there oil in them there hills? The D'Arcy Exploration Co. certainly thought there might be when they began a test bore in March 1936, causing the quiet hillside above Paulsgrove to become a scene of feverish activity as a miniature mining village sprang up around the 136-foot-high derrick tower. A borehole over a mile deep was driven into the hillside, traces of oil were found, but not in sufficient quantities to justify further drilling, and the venture was abandoned in February 1937. (PCM)

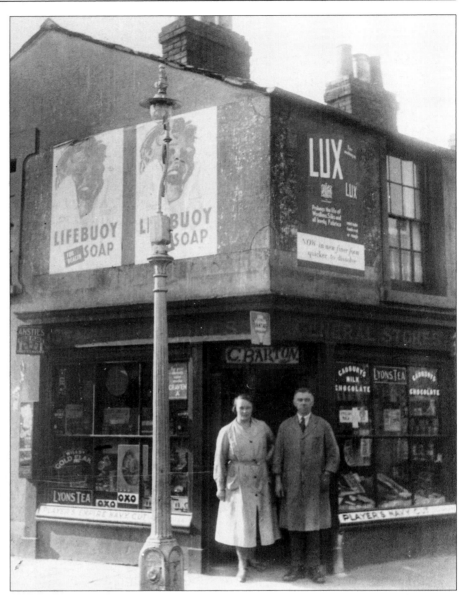

Charles and Annie Barton outside their shop at 130 Crasswell Street, Landport, on the corner with Cottage View, about 1937. The Bartons ran a classic corner shop, selling a wide range of goods, often in pennyworths, and giving credit to reliable customers. The shop was destroyed by wartime bombing.

(H/1999/349)

'The Home on the Beach' – as described in the 1933 official guide to Southsea. 'Here is the perfect home on the beach, within a few feet of the beach and with turf paths in front, into which everything can go – the pails, buckets, bathing wraps, towels and the hamper of good things for lunch.' And it reminds us that at the end of the day 'one can avoid all that fatigue of carrying back the paraphenalia ...', all except the hamper of course 'which must go back for replenishment for the morrow'. The guide then exhorts us to 'Observe this jolly family party, all active and interested, for in the Solent there is a constant procession of liners and battleships intriguing to the dweller inland'. (PCM)

Children's Corner, Southsea, sited where the Sea Life Centre now stands. This playground was once a Mecca for children of all ages, providing amongst other things boating and paddling pools, a slide, sandpits and a miniature train '... with a real steam locomotive, a real engine driver and a real station. What more could children desire?'

(1158/1987)

Clarence Pier, Southsea, c. 1936. By the mid-1930s, when this photograph was taken, visitors to Clarence Pier could enjoy dancing in the circular Pavilion Ballroom or take refreshment in the spacious cafes ranged around the sun deck. The high scaffold of the roller coaster ride at Butlin's amusement park was a familiar landmark for passengers approaching the pier on the paddle steamers which plied daily to and from the Isle of Wight.

(1518A/1/40ph)

Hilsea Lido was opened on 25 July 1935. The 1930s cult for healthy living was enthusiastically taken up by Portsmouth corporation with the creation of Hilsea Lido in the north of the city. It was constructed in the most modern style and remains today as a fine example of Art Deco design. As well as the swimming pool complex there were formal gardens, tennis courts, a boating lake and restaurants all with panoramic views of Portsdown Hill, the creek and the upper reaches of the harbour. (DL/P220)

King George V's Silver Jubilee in 1935 gave the whole country an opportunity for celebrations. In Portsmouth, street parties on a lavish scale were organised for 6 May. Entertainments continued throughout the week, culminating with free admission for 25,000 children into the local cinemas on Saturday. Here suitably-bedecked helpers take time out from their tasks to have their photograph taken in Aylesbury Road, Buckland.

(481/1993)

Coronation Carnival 15 May 1937. The coronation of George VI gave Portsmouth people another excuse to get out the bunting and parade through the streets in celebration.

(1409A/5/3ii)

Mudlarks at the Hard, about 1937. In the past the children of Portsea would entreat passers-by to throw a penny in the mud which they would then dive down and retrieve – hence the name 'mudlarks'. Although 'mudlarking' was frowned upon as a form of begging, these youngsters seem to be doing it more for fun than necessity.

(513/1993)

Dancing, glamorised by Fred Astaire and Ginger Rodgers, was an immensely popular pastime in the '30s. Here the Portsmouth Amateur Ballroom Formation Dancing Team pose for the photographer at the Esplanade Assembly Rooms, Southsea, after winning the Southern Region Competition Cup for the slow foxtrot in 1938. Ivy Anthony, as she was then, on the extreme left, went on to establish the Ivy Hadley School of Dancing where many local people learnt the intricacies of ballroom dancing in the years following the Second World War. (H/186/94)

Fans of Portsmouth Football Club fill Guildhall Square to welcome home their heroes. On Saturday, 29 April 1939 Pompey beat Wolverhampton Wanderers 4-1 to win the FA Cup. Due to the intervention of the war Portsmouth held the cup for six consecutive years – a record, as yet, still unbeaten!

(Courtesy of *The News*, 567A/2/18)

The Highbury estate, c. 1934. '... as recently as 1928 waving fields of corn, bridle paths and moorlands met the eye where now stands the charming and up-to-date suburb of Highbury'. These sentiments quoted from an article printed in the *Portsmouth Evening News* about 1934 are born out by these two contrasting photographs showing Hawthorn Crescent as construction began and the estate as it looked a few years later when muddy paths were making way for tar and concrete. (307/1993 & DA/2/B/598)

Fire at Fratton Co-op, Friday, 20 July 1934. The fire began in the records room where, it is believed, intense sunlight shining through a skylight caused the papers to ignite. The fire spread with amazing rapidity and despite the combined efforts of the city fire brigade and the dockyard fire service, within an hour and a half there was only brickwork and masonry left. Despite the fact that the fire occurred around 10.30 am on a busy Friday morning there were, suprisingly, no casualties reported. (1603A/11/2)

Mrs Price in the kitchen of 2 Wisborough Road, Southsea, about 1938. A scene typical in many households – mum making cakes for the family – no boxes of shop bought fancies in those days! In fact Mrs Price had been widowed, leaving her to bring up two young boys alone on a limited income. (466/1993)

Gas Mask Drill, Wymering 1939. Air raid precautions began as early as 1938 and before the outbreak of war the following year 38 million gas masks had been issued to every man, woman and child in Britain. Gas masks were often viewed with dislike and even fear by children and so this enterprising warden in Wymering has organised a drill and made it FUN by introducing an accordion player to the proceedings and giving the occasion a carnival atmosphere.

(Courtesy of *The News*)

The evacuation of children from cities around the country in 1939 was the largest movement of people ever seen in Britain. In order to get it 'right on the day' Portsmouth City Council organised a mock evacuation on 27 July 1939 when 900 school children were transported from George Street School in 14 corporation buses. They are seen here in the goods yard at Greetham Street awaiting to board trains at Portsmouth and Southsea Station.

(Courtesy of *The News*)

What were you doing the day war broke out? Ivy Anthony, now Ivy Tibbles, was amongst the many that answered the appeal in the *Portsmouth Evening News* for 'a considerable number of volunteers to fill sandbags' at Eastney Esplanade for protecting public buildings and making temporary shelters. (H/186/94)

In the centre of Portsmouth where the erection of Anderson shelters was difficult the council built communal shelters in the streets. These workmen are assembling a pre-cast concrete shelter in Commercial Road, ready to be covered in soil or concrete.

(Courtesy of The News)

1940 – 1949

Volunteers preparing ration books and coupons at the Northern Secondary School in Mayfield Road in October 1939. One hundred volunteers produced 260,000 ration books by the time food rationing began in January 1940.

(Courtesy of *The News*, WS208A)

The threat of a German invasion led to the closure of Southsea seafront on 4 July 1940. In this photograph amusement machines are being crated up and removed from South Parade Pier.

(Courtesy of *The News*, WS930)

Bomb damage to the Blue Anchor Hotel and adjoining properties at Kingston Cross resulting from the first German air raid on Portsmouth. Eighteen people were killed in this daylight raid on 11 July 1940. (BB30)

A German aerial reconnaissance photograph of Portsmouth taken in August 1940. Potential bombing targets have been marked, including railways, barracks, *HMS Dolphin*, the power station and various features in the dockyard. (PMRS)

A single German 2500 kg 'Max' bomb, dropped on the night of 23-24 December 1940, caused widespread destruction and killed 18 people in the Conway Street area of Landport.

(Courtesy of *The News*, WS1310)

The interior of the Guildhall after it was destroyed by incendiary bombs on the night of 10-11 January 1941. This major German 'blitz' on Portsmouth left 171 people dead, 430 injured and 3000 homeless.

(BB5)

A number of the victims of the 10 January raid were buried in a public funeral at Kingston cemetery on 17 January 1941. A total of 930 civilians and many service personnel died in Portsmouth during the war through enemy action.

(Courtesy of *The News*, WS1353)

The Prime Minister, Winston Churchill, visited Portsmouth on 31 January 1941 to inspect the bomb damage. In this photograph he is shaking hands with George Smith, who at sixteen was the youngest worker in the dockyard.

(Courtesy of the Imperial War Museum, H6946)

On 6 February 1941 the King and Queen toured the bombed areas of the city with the Lord Mayor, Denis Daley, and his wife. Councillor Daley served as Lord Mayor from 1939 to 1944. He was knighted for his services to civil defence in June 1941.

(Courtesy of *The News*, WS1395)

German bombs destroyed many notable buildings in the High Street on 10 January 1941, but the Cathedral survived. Admiral James, the Commander-in-Chief, Portsmouth later wrote, 'To many the sight of this majestic and unscarred building rising above acres of rubble was an inspiration'. (BC15)

King's Road, Southsea, was extensively damaged in the Blitz. On the left, in the distance, can be seen the North Block of Clarence Barracks, now the City Museum and Records Office. (H/50/95)

Mrs Mitchard at the entrance to 'The Glory 'Ole', as this ARP (Air Raid Precautions) Wardens' Post was nicknamed. It was in the basement of Mr and Mrs Mitchard's hair-dresser's shop in Jessie Road, off Fawcett Road. In November 1940 there were 560 full-time and 1228 part-time ARP Wardens in Portsmouth. (472/1998)

Civil Defence Rescue and Demolition Squads such as this came under the City Engineer's Department, and included skilled men from the construction industry. Their most difficult job was to rescue people trapped in blitzed buildings. Between air raids they made safe or pulled down damaged houses and recovered people's possessions. (73/1995/3)

Ambulance drivers and first aiders at ARP Depot No 5, Kent Street School, Portsea, in September 1939.

(53/1985/3)

An anti-aircraft gun site was established on Southsea Common in 1939, consisting of four 4.5-inch guns. They were manned by 214 (Southsea) Battery of the 57th (Wessex) Heavy Anti-Aircraft Regiment. Autumn rains turned the site into a quagmire. (562/1997)

Identity cards being checked at Portsmouth and Southsea Railway Station in the lead up to D-Day in 1944. As a security measure a complete ban on non-residents entering a coastal belt ten miles deep from Land's End to the Wash was imposed on 1 April.

(Courtesy of *The News*, WS2823)

This photograph shows concrete caissons under construction in the dockyard in January 1944. These 'Phoenix' units were to form part of the breakwaters for the artificial 'Mulberry' harbours the Allies planned to take with them when they invaded Normandy.

(Courtesy of the Imperial War Museum, H35371)

Troops leaving for Normandy in 1944 from South Parade Pier. The scaffolding walkway was constructed to create a 'one-way' system for loading and unloading landing craft. In 1948 the D-Day memorial stone was unveiled close to the pier to commemorate Portsmouth's role in the preparations for Operation OVERLORD.

(Courtesy of *The News*, WS2945)

The Plotting Room in the Combined Operations headquarters below Fort Southwick on Portsdown Hill. In 1944 cross-channel movements for the invasion of Normandy were controlled from this headquarters. The plaque over the plotting table is now on display at the D-Day Museum in Southsea. It bears the unofficial coat of arms of the plotting room staff and the motto - 'This Blessed Plot'.

(Courtesy of *The News*, WS3213A)

A German V1 flying bomb hit Newcomen Road, Stamshaw, on 15 July 1944. It resulted in 15 deaths and 82 injuries. Two 'doodlebugs' landed on Portsmouth. The first, in Locksway Road, caused no fatalities.

(Courtesy of *The News*, WS2956)

Clearance of bombed buildings in Hyde Park Road in September 1943. Planning for the rebuilding of Portsmouth had begun in February 1941.

(608A/5)

The Home Guard stood down in November 1944. The farewell parade for 3000 men of the Home Guard in Portsmouth took place on 3 December 1944. (620/1998)

This bonfire of black-out material and air raid shelter mattresses at Hilltop Crescent was lit to celebrate the end of the war in Europe in May 1945.

(50/1985/2)

8 May 1945 was officially declared Victory-in-Europe (VE) Day and street parties were held all over Portsmouth. This photograph was taken in Essex Road, Milton.

(104/1995/5)

Victory-over-Japan (VJ) Day brought the Second World War to an end on 15 August 1945. It was an occasion for further celebrations and street parties. This one took place in Silverlock Street.

(121/1996)

Prefabricated bungalows on the slopes of Portsdown Hill. The first 'pre-fabs' were ready in July 1945, and by 1947 the City Council had erected more than 700 of them.

(138A/9/2)

This photograph shows Diane and Irene Goldsmith playing in Deerhurst Crescent, Paulsgrove, about 1949. Work on building the new housing estates in Paulsgrove and Wymering began in February 1946. The new estates at Leigh Park were begun in September 1947.

(316/1995)

This rather strange photograph, taken on 8 December 1947, shows an experiment with an illuminated police point duty stand at the junction of Commercial Road and Edinburgh Road. A policeman had recently been seriously injured while on point duty near the dog track. The Chief Constable told the City Accident Prevention Council that he hoped eventually to have both fixed and mobile illuminated stands across the city.

(PMRS)

Portsmouth Football Club ended the 1948-49 season as League Division I champions. In this photograph taken at Fratton Park, the Captain, Reg Flewin, is holding the trophy and beside him is the club president, Field Marshal Montgomery. 'Monty' had accepted an invitation to become president while on a visit to Portsmouth in March 1944. The club won the league again the following season. (Courtesy of *The News*, 23/1994)

Not everyone welcomed the creation of the NHS in 1948. This float was photographed during a fête at the Queen Alexandra Hospital, probably early that year. The QA accepted its first civilian patients during the war. (5/1996)

1950 – 1959

Portsmouth Synagogue, The Thicket, Southsea.   A Jewish community existed in the town as early as the 1730s and according to tradition the first synagogue was then in a rented room in Oyster Street.   It later moved to White's Row, Portsea, before the present synagogue was opened in 1936.   In 1951 the synagogue was reconsecrated by the Commonwealth's Chief Rabbi, following repairs after wartime damage.   (Courtesy of J.A. Hewes, 149/1977)

Couples take to the floor at this Portsmouth dance class run by Ivy Hadley, about 1950. It would not be long before 'rock n' roll' would begin to offer an alternative to this more traditional form of dancing. (H/186/1994)

St Jude's church, Southsea, Centenary Service in 1951. Built by Thomas Ellis Owen to serve the growing Southsea of the nineteenth century, the church remains a focal point of the area today. (137/1976)

Fratton Bridge from the corner of Selbourne Terrace early in the 1950s.

(Courtesy of Wright & Logan, V7)

St George's Maltings, St George's Square, Portsea, 1953. These maltings belonged to Portsmouth United Breweries, one of the larger companies in Portsmouth's important brewing industry. In 1953 United merged with Brickwood's, and the maltings, damaged in the war, were demolished to make way for workshops. (BP69)

Commercial Road, looking north from the corner of Church Street, on a summer's morning in 1953. Redevelopment had yet to begin in this section of Commercial Road, but today the scene is very different, with a busy dual carriageway leading to the M275. The Savoy Cinema on the corner of Fitzherbert Street is now the ABC Cinema, while the site of the Country House pub is part of the car park opposite.   (L138)

A summer morning market day in Commercial Road, 1953, looking north towards All Saints Church. The traffic congestion caused by the wholesale vegetable market was one reason why the Tricorn Centre was built.   (L39)

Portsmouth North End Cycling Club on a club run at Portsbridge in 1952. Cycling and rambling clubs were particularly popular at this time. A police box with an officer on duty is on the right of the photograph.   (PCM)

Two children share the limelight at this coronation street party in Aylesbury Road, Buckland, in 1953.

(484/1993)

A day out on the swings by St Francis' Vicarage, Riders Lane, Leigh Park, near Havant about 1953. The estate was built on land bought by the city in 1944, to help re-house Portsmouth's population after the war. (AE40)

Rebuilding and road widening work underway in Arundel Street in 1952, looking towards Commercial Road. Lloyds Bank faces Arundel Street. Reynolds' wallpaper shop takes shape behind the scaffolding. (M23)

King's Road was heavily bombed during the war and much rebuilding was necessary. In this view, taken early in the 1950s, newly-built council flats can be seen along both sides of King's Road. The ruins of St Paul's church still stand in St Paul's Square, and the chimney of Portsmouth and Brighton United Breweries Ltd can be seen close by. Victoria Barracks sits imposingly on the corner of Alexandra Road and King's Terrace. (6961/3)

Broad Street and Point, Old Portsmouth, in 1955. The slipway for the Isle of Wight ferries can be seen at the end of Broad Street, while the cranes of Vosper's shipyard tower over the Camber. Opposite them, the coal bunkers of Fraser and White Ltd lie alongside Town Quay. The north-west side of the High Street from the Cathedral to Broad Street has been cleared of its bomb damaged buildings, but the remains of the porticoed city museum can just be made out opposite St Thomas's. (154A/4/1)

The area around the burnt-out Guildhall in 1955, with bomb sites still clearly visible. Victoria Baths have been completed, while the building of the telephone exchange, in Park Road, is in progress. The buildings seen here in St Michael's Road would later disappear with redevelopment. St Michael's church and the Royal Navy and Royal Marines Orphans Home were demolished in the 1960s with the advent of a new road layout, while St Andrew's church at the other end of the road closed in 1984. (54A/5)

The extent of the damage to Portsmouth's Guildhall is revealed here, as rebuilding work begins in 1955. Four years later the Queen officially opened the newly finished building. (109A/6/22/2)

Sir Adrian Boult lays the foundation stone of the John Pounds Unitarian Church in High Street, Portsmouth, on 24 September 1955. Built on the site of the former Unitarian Chapel, this new church marked the union of the High Street Presbyterian Chapel and the General Baptist Chapel in St Thomas Street, which were both destroyed in 1941. (CHU82/12/4)

The Admiral of the Soviet Baltic Fleet and the captain of the Russian cruiser *Ordzhonikdz*, arriving to visit Lord Mayor George Day at the city council offices at Western Parade, Southsea, in 1956. Ships of the Russian fleet were in Portsmouth as part of Nikita Kruschev's official visit to Britain. The Russians later accused Britain of underwater espionage against their ships while in Portsmouth. The mysterious death of British naval frogman, Commander Crabb, at the same time as the Russian visit fuelled speculation that he was responsible. (82A/5)

A typical seaside view of the 1950s, as people enjoy a stroll along Southsea Esplanade east of South Parade Pier.

(Courtesy of Wright & Logan, DL/P138)

As the 1950s progressed women's fashion changed radically, with trousers and shorts becoming increasingly popular. Here the new mixes with the old at Clarence Pier in 1955, before the pier's entertainment complex was rebuilt after wartime bombing.

(PCRO)

A young girl rides her tricycle around a tranquil Ladies Mile, Southsea.

(Courtesy of Wright & Logan, DL/P114)

Southsea Miniature Railway and children's paddling pool. A favourite spot in the 1950s. The Sealife Centre now occupies the site. (Courtesy of *The News*, PCRO)

Roller Skating Rink, Southsea. Proudly proclaimed as the largest open air rink at the time, the rink was widely used by the public as well as for competitions and demonstrations. The old bandstand building forms the centre of the rink, as it still does today, with the rink now a skateboarding park. (PCRO)

The one that didn't get away! But still a disappointed young Southsea angler. (DL/P63)

The George Inn on Portsdown Hill in the late 1950s. (AF20)

The A3 London Road, looking south from Portsbridge in 1956. Northern Parade stretches away to the right. The moat is clearly visible in the foreground, as well as the fort-like Bastion restaurant, using the old defences for some effective advertising. Beyond is the Southdown bus garage, with its later barrel-vaulted extension on the other side of the road. The original depot is now used by the Co-operative Dairies, while the Provincial Bus Company operates from the site opposite.

(AF19)

The adult pool at Hilsea Lido in 1959, showing diving tower, cascades at each end, and water chute. Opened in 1935, the Lido was built to provide safe and enjoyable bathing in the north of the city as an alternative to Southsea beach. (Courtesy of Wright & Logan, DL/P99)

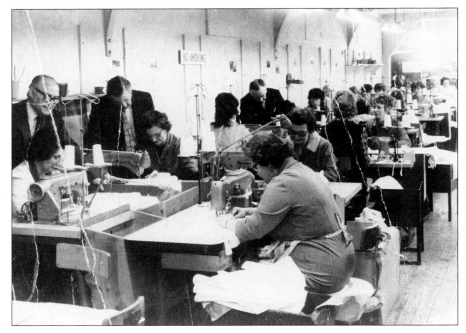

Workers at the Surrey Street factory of corset manufacturer Chilcot and Williams. Portsmouth's specialisation in the corset making industry in the second half of the nineteenth century and the beginning of the twentieth, was unrivalled throughout the country. One of the foremost firms was Chilcot and Williams, founded in 1869. The company survived for nearly a century, but after T. P. Williams death in 1962 it was taken over by Berlei (UK) Ltd in 1965. The factory in Surrey Street finally closed in 1970. (377/1997)

The steam-powered floating bridge between Portsmouth and Gosport began service in 1840. It was operated by chains which were drawn up as the ferry crossed and then dropped to the seabed to avoid impeding vessels using the harbour. By the 1950s the bridge had largely been superseded by the diesel passenger ferry and in December 1959 the service was abandoned. The *Alexandra*, seen here unloading at Broad Street, ran most services during the 1950s, no mean feat as she had started crossings in 1864! (D107)

The Isle of Wight paddle steamer *Sandown*, berthed near the harbour station with the motor vessels Brading and Southsea alongside.

(1712A/1/1/20)

Candy the elephant being enticed aboard the Isle of Wight car ferry, watched by an amused crowd, on the Broad Street slipway in March 1959. (1712A/2/1/60 6)

Workers streaming out of the main dockyard gate. The masts of *HMS Victory* stand out clearly. (DL/P59)

Carols around the Christmas tree in Portsmouth's Anglican Cathedral.

(Courtesy of *The News*, CHU2/6/54/10)

1960 – 1969

Princess Alexandra, standing left, opening a new building for St George's Church of England School, Portsea, 29 October 1962. The 1960s were an important time for education in Portsmouth, seeing the opening of Highbury College in 1962, the decision to make the secondary school system comprehensive, in 1969, and the college of technology becoming a polytechnic in 1969. (CHU2/4/12/15/7)

Sports day at Milton school, 1966. (CHU47/2G/4/10)

A social evening for members of Young Labour in 1960. The fashion revolution of the '60s has not yet begun: the girls' dresses are padded out with stiff petticoats, while the boys wear baggy trousers, not jeans or drainpipes, and have short hair.

(1470A/9/15/13)

Miss Paulsgrove, 1961. The new estate at Paulsgrove rapidly developed a strong community life.

(Courtesy of *The News*, 9491, PCRO)

A policewoman, about 1960. Portsmouth's police force, established in 1836, was amalgamated with the Hampshire force on 1 April 1967.

(42/1980)

In the early 1960s beauty contests were a popular entertainment on South Parade Pier. The girls are approaching the stage at the seaward end of the pier, led by a short man with a pink parasol. Photos of the competitions appeared in the resort's tourist guides. Cheap package holidays to sunnier places undermined the British seaside holiday, however, and during the 1970s the emphasis in Portsmouth's publicity switched to its historic heritage.   (DL/P382)

Air hostesses Diana Hart-Thomas and her colleague Sylvia at Portsmouth airfield in 1962. Channel Airways began flying to the Channel Islands from Portsmouth in 1955, but left the city after two of its aircraft crashed on landing on 15 August 1967. The grass runways were not long enough when wet for aircraft big enough to be economic to fly, and the airport had to close in 1973.

(H/1999/357)

The winter of 1962-1963 was particularly long and hard. These boys are walking on the ice covering the moat of Hilsea Lines, just to the east of Portsbridge, in January 1963.

(Courtesy of *The News*, PCRO)

Christmas shoppers in Commercial Road, 1964. In the background is the Landport Drapery Bazaar, renamed Allders in 1982. The LDB, a department store, was founded in 1865. It was destroyed by German bombs on the night of 10 January 1941, and this building was erected in the early 1950s after Commercial Road and Arundel Street had been widened.   (K13)

Commercial Road was closed for three weeks in February 1967 and again in April to see whether a pedestrian precinct would be successful. This was the second of the two experiments, when buses continued to use the thoroughfare.   (PCRO slide)

The northern end of Cosham High Street, photographed in December 1966.

(AB38)

This photo of Queen Street, taken opposite the entrance to Cuzon Howe Road in March 1962, demonstrates how people of all ages relied on bicycles before car ownership became widespread. The eighteenth-century thoroughfare was widened in 1968-1970 by the demolition of the Georgian and Victorian buildings on the north side of the street that had survived wartime bombing.

(C90a)

Commercial Road near the Continental Café, November 1965. The number of cars on Portsmouth's roads more than doubled between 1955 and 1964 and was expected to keep rising fast, so the council created an inner ring road around the Guildhall area. The buildings on the right were demolished to make way for this scheme not long after this photo was taken.

(E181)

Demolition in progress in the Lake Road area in 1963. Several hundred houses and businesses here were redeveloped in the early 1960s, including the chemist's shop run by Lawrence Snellgrove, who took this picture. They were replaced mostly by blocks of flats. (332/1994/3)

Redevelopment of aged housing was a dominant theme of Portsmouth's history in the 1950s and 1960s. Centre left in this photo, taken in October 1968, are the cleared streets of the Seymour and Arnaud Close district. Centre right are the terraced streets of western Buckland and the line of the old northern end of Commercial Road, the last area of Portsmouth to be comprehensively redeveloped rather than improved. (PCM)

Wartime bombing was not wholly responsible for the changes to central Portsmouth visible by 1968. On the left are the high-rise blocks of Somerstown, erected in the late 1950s and early '60s. In front of them is St Luke's School, begun in 1962. To the school's right are the central police station, finished 1959, while the nearby law courts and art college were both completed in 1960. A swathe of land has been left clear for the dual carriageway now called Winston Churchill Way, while the long-delayed Guildhall Square redevelopment was about to transform the bombsites south of the station. (PCM)

Augusto Verrecchia (universally known as 'Tony'), an immigrant from Italy, opened his popular café in 1933. The ice cream served was made downstairs, always with the best ingredients available. This photo was taken in June 1966. The building was compulsorily purchased when the Civic Offices were constructed and closed in 1970. The Verrecchia family still makes ice cream under the name Verrossi, and runs a café in North End. (F21A)

The Tricorn Centre in April 1966, shortly before it was officially opened. There were to be 48 shops, a supermarket and a department store, while the city's wholesale fruit and vegetable market was to be held on the first floor. The architect, Owen Luder, intended it should have the atmosphere of a casbah. A recession began just as it was finished, however, few shops were let and the building decayed, attracting increasing dislike among local people. Demolition is due to start in 1999.

(Courtesy of *The News*, DA/2/B/162)

Navy Days in the dockyard, early in the 1960s. In the background on the right is the huge 250-ton cantilever crane in No. 3 Basin, built in 1912 and demolished in 1984. In 1968 the industrial side of the dockyard employed 8500 people, while some 25,000 altogether worked in Admiralty establishments in the Portsmouth area. (DL/P 384)

Southsea Castle after the army had gone. With the development of missiles there was no need for gun batteries to defend the dockyard. Portsmouth ceased to have a military garrison in 1961, while the government sold to the council the Round Tower, Point Battery, Long Curtain and King's Bastion in 1958, and Square Tower and Southsea Castle in 1960. The castle opened as a museum in 1967. (DA2/B/1227)

The Lord Mayor's car is ceremoniously driven aboard the *MV Fishbourne* on its inaugural voyage to the Isle of Wight, 7 July 1961. This new vessel could carry 34 cars and 168 passengers. It replaced the ferry of the same name in service on the route to Fishbourne since 1927. At the same time the ferry terminus was moved from the end of Broad Street to the eastern side of Point.

(1712A/2/1/7)

A publicity photo taken for a tourist brochure, about 1966. The hovercraft service to the Isle of Wight began operating from here in 1965, having started in 1964 at Eastney. The rebuilding of Clarence Pier, bombed in January 1941, began in 1953. It was reopened on 1 June 1961. (DL/P318)

Alec Rose, a Southsea greengrocer, set off from Langstone Harbour to sail around the world single-handed on 16 July 1967. His return on 4 July 1968 was a triumph witnessed by a quarter-of-a-million people. The following day it was announced that he was to be knighted for his achievement. (9187/16)

Jim Callaghan was born in Portsmouth in 1912. He joined the civil service and became a trade unionist before becoming an MP in 1945. Lord Callaghan is the only man ever to have held the four principal offices of state, being Chancellor of the Exchequer 1964-67, Home Secretary 1967-70, Foreign Secretary 1974-76 and Prime Minister 1976-79. (1470A/9/15/15)

The Queen accepting the keys of the City of Portsmouth at Portsmouth and Southsea Station on 16 May 1969. Her Majesty had come to review a combined NATO fleet of 63 vessels from 12 countries. (Courtesy of *The News*, PCRO)

Until 1967 the A3 crossed the summit of Portsdown Hill to the west of the George Inn. That year the road was moved into a cutting east of the pub, and a bridge built over it. This bulldozer was used to create the new earthworks, but why the one of the city's photographers snapped several pictures of this blonde with it is unknown. She is wearing a bell-sleeved mini dress typical of the period, with a pattern in turquoise and green, fashionable colours. The driver is wearing denim jeans, which had just become common as casual wear as well as for dirty work. (PCRO slide)

In April 1969 work was at last in progress on the South Coast Trunk Road, now known as the M27 and A27. This view shows the new roundabout and bridge widening at Portsbridge, while the foundations of the new road stretch away eastwards. Between the roadworks and the Highbury estate, a suburban development of the 1930s, are the buildings of Highbury Technical College, opened in 1963. The multistorey maths and science block opened in 1966. (PCRO slide)

Twyford Avenue, September 1969. This street became one-way in 1966, but traffic problems continued until the building of the M275. The motorway was originally routed down Twyford Avenue, but popular pressure defeated the plan.

(DA2/B/1336)

This huge hole at Eastney, photographed in June 1968, was part of major improvements to the city's sewer system carried out between 1965 and 1973. New deep sewers were dug, largely by mechanical mole, up the east side of the island, and through Southsea and then north to Stamshaw. (PCRO slide)

The Camber, looking across to Vosper's shipyard, April 1969. Vospers was a long-established shipbuilding company, having begun as engine-building specialists in 1872. In 1966 they merged with John I. Thornycroft, shipbuilders in Southampton. The yard in the Camber was closed late in 1985. Redevelopment of the site for housing was suspended in the late 1980s because of a recession, but 'King James Quay' is now complete.

(D12)

In the early 1960s the council decided to build as much new housing as it could within the city boundaries. Inevitably much of it had to be flats, and central government subsidies for flats were bigger than for houses. Portsdown Park, here pictured in May 1969, was begun in 1968 to designs chosen through an architectural competition. The buildings suffered so badly from water penetration that in 1987 their demolition was begun.

(AF17)

1970–1979

Access to Portsmouth was dramatically improved in the early 1970s by the construction of the M275 motorway. The foundations of the road, cutting through the south-western corner of Stamshaw, are clear in this photo taken in September 1972. Buildings still line Commercial Road, but were soon to be demolished as part of the scheme. The Rudmore gasholder and park on the site of the former Portsea Island General Cemetery have become part of the ferryport.

(336/72/3b)

Fratton Bridge in August 1970, looking south into Victoria Road North.

(114/70/8)

The economy of the city was boosted in the 1970s by the arrival of new industries and companies. An area in the north of Portsmouth Harbour was reclaimed and the new UK headquarters for IBM built there. (DA/2/B/642/1)

This photo taken in 1977 shows the Zurich Insurance Company's newly completed building. This building transformed the site of the old *Portsmouth Evening News* offices and the company brought much-needed jobs to the city.

(DA/2/B/1436/1)

The decision was taken by the city council to expand the commercial ferry port and the building of new berths opened up Portsmouth to the lucrative cross-channel ferry trade. These two photographs show the beginnings of the work and one of the finished berths. Amidst all of the change the old Rudmore Cellars public house still remains.

(DA/2/B/259/1 and DA/2/B/270/1)

When Kingston Crescent was first built up it was lined by imposing houses. Changes in society meant that these houses, which had been constructed in the days when most middle-class families had servants, had deteriorated badly and by the 1970s many were sold and awaiting demolition. (DA/2/B/694/3)

Halfway along Kingston Crescent was Kingston House. Having fallen into disrepair some years before, it was demolished in the mid-1970s, a sad end for a house that had been home to a city alderman, a major-general and other well-to-do families. (DC/2/B/694/2)

The 1970s saw the reconstruction of the Guildhall Square and surrounding roads. Whilst some areas had been heavily bombed during the Second World War other parts had to be cleared by the bulldozers as here in the Russell Street area, which had been home to small shops and businesses. (DA/2/B/520/1)

In 1973 the Guildhall Square became one large building site as work started on what was to become the Civic Offices. (DA/2/B/203/1)

As part of the new Guildhall Square complex a new central library formed the south-eastern corner. The library had occupied part of the old Municipal College since 1908. This photo was taken in 1974.

(DA/2/B/153/44)

In June 1972 traffic still flowed through Commercial Road and shoppers had to brave the buses and cars as they went from shop to shop.

(PCRO)

By the summer of 1972 work on the pedestrianisation of Commercial Road had started although in this photograph the workmen seem more interested in enjoying the summer sunshine. W. H. Smith were still on the corner of Crasswell Street with Bishop Bros shoe shop next door. (DA/2/B/235/3)

Commercial Road as most of us know it and with a wide variety of fashions shown – flared trousers, mini-skirts and hot pants. This photo was taken in August 1972.

(DA/2/B/235/4)

The finished precinct proved popular with shoppers, but it was to be some time before it was extended south to encompass Arundel Street and the Edinburgh Road junction.

(DA/2/B/235/1)

The fountain given by Allders Ltd to commemorate the Silver Jubilee of 1977 and the extension of the precinct to Arundel Street and Edinburgh Road give us the road layout that we know in 1998, a far cry from the traffic-congested road of the earlier part of the century. This picture was taken on 4 August 1978. (DA/2/B/241/1)

The only remaining part of the original Commercial Road shopping area was the Charlotte Street market. In this photograph taken in 1971 some of the shops which disappeared with the building of the Cascades Centre can still be seen, such as Frank's, Shirt King and the Market Snack Bar.

(DA/2/B/162/1)

The hovercraft service from Portsmouth to Ryde had started in 1965 and is the oldest regular passenger service in the world. In 1972 on Saturday 4 March a SRN6 hovercraft en route from Ryde to Southsea capsized only 400 yards from the shore. The freak wind and sea conditions which were held to blame resulted in the death of five passengers. Thankfully 22 people were rescued. (DA/2/B/1320/1)

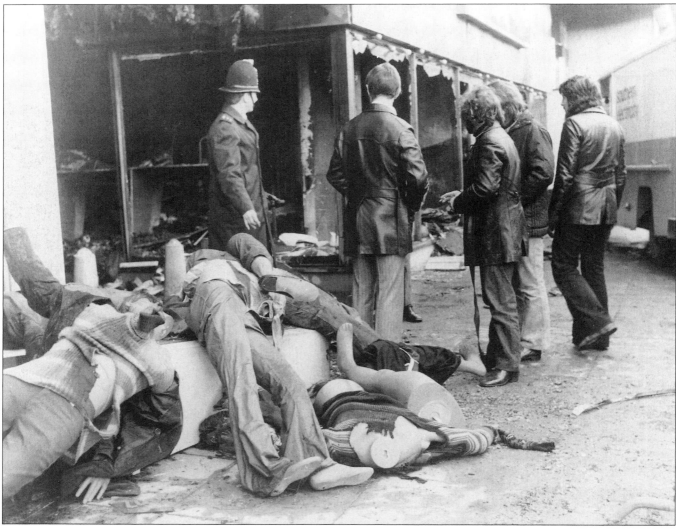

Fire affected various well-known buildings in the city during this decade. In this photograph part of the Tricorn shopping complex was damaged. The dummies show the remains of the flared trousers and striped jumpers that were then fashionable. (DA/2/B/1327/1)

The old Ebenezer Methodist Church in Twyford Avenue had been redundant for some years and used as a wholesale depot by Benney & Sons. The building caught fire in February 1971 and was eventually demolished. In the extreme left of the photograph it is possible to see one of the fine old houses that used to line Twyford Avenue and Commercial Road.

(DA/2/B/1337/1)

During the summer of 1974 the film producer Ken Russell filmed *Tommy* in Southsea. South Parade Pier, which he used as a location, caught fire during filming. Ironically the first South Parade Pier had burnt down in 1904, now its successor had suffered the same fate.

(Local History slides, BH12)

When the fire had been brought under control, only a burn-out shell was left. (DA/2/B/1216/3)

The theatre on the pier had hosted many summer shows, but all that remained after the fire was the proscenium arch. (DA/2/B/1216/1)

A baker's strike in 1974 resulted in queues outside the independent bakers reminiscent of wartime. This queue at Cosham in December 1974 was typical of many throughout the city. This photograph and several others in this section were taken by the late R. F. Reynolds, a gifted local amateur photographer.   (R. F. Reynolds Collection)

The newspaper seller was once a common sight on our city streets but now few remain. This gentleman selling papers in the High Street at Cosham was well-known in the area.   (R. F. Reynolds Collection)

The Droke, a narrow lane running from the High Street at Cosham is the setting for this atmospheric scene. Although reminiscent of the 'Dixon of Dock Green' image of the police force, this was in fact taken in 1971.   (R. F. Reynolds Collection)

The Queen's Silver Jubilee in 1977 led to celebrations throughout the city. Her Majesty visited the city on 29 June 1977 and was greeted by the Lord Mayor and City Council in the Guildhall Square. This photo demonstrates how the new square was designed to form an arena for such public occasions. (DA/2/B/1050/4)

The crowds lining the street outside the old General Post Office provide a vivid contrast to the formality of the civic welcome, with some members of the crowd more flamboyantly dressed than others!

(DA/2/B/1050/3)

This is Fratton Road looking north, with the Wesley Central Hall on the right, decorated for the Silver Jubilee. (DA/2/B/1050/1)

A competition for the best dressed street resulted in many unusual ideas. The owners of this house transformed their garage door into a Union Jack. (DA/2/B/1050/20)

Street parties were held throughout the city, here the entertainment is in full swing in Essex Road as Shazam play. (R. F. Reynolds Collection)

A review of the fleet took place at Spithead in June 1977, providing opportunities for many small craft to tour the assembled ships.

(R. F. Reynolds Collection)

Southsea skate park was opened by the Lord Mayor, Cllr G. H. Austin, on 11 June 1978. A bye-law prohibited skateboarders using pavements and roads, which led to success for the park. The original 1920s bandstand still remains within the new facilities. Activities at the park include roller skating, skateboarding, BMX biking and street hockey.

(160/78/29)

1980 – 1989

An informal gathering outside the Charles Dickens' Birthplace Museum in June 1980 marked the completion of work to beautify the precinct in which it stands. Present were children from the Charles Dickens' Middle School, members of the Portsmouth branch of the Dickens Fellowship, councillors and the City Planning Officer. The work, partly funded by a worldwide appeal by the fellowship, included planting trees and putting a blue plaque on the house.

(113/80/5)

In 1666 Charles II appointed a Dutch military engineer, Sir Bernard de Gomme, to build fortifications around Portsmouth. This photograph shows the surviving works he designed. The bridge over the moat leads from a tunnel through Long Curtain, on the left, to Spur Redoubt, jutting into the sea on the right. The redoubt has since been excavated and the promenade taken over it on a footbridge.

(35/80/1c)

In 1545 the *Mary Rose*, pride of Henry VIII's navy, sank off Portsmouth with a loss of some seven hundred men. In 1981, following extensive excavation, the ship was brought to the surface and transported to her new home in the dockyard. Prince Charles, who was actively involved in the project, still takes a keen interest in the ship's conservation, and the progress of the Mary Rose Museum.

(DA/2/B/1/788)

This photograph depicts Fort Purbrook, which is situated between Fort Widley and Farlington Redoubt. The construction of the forts started in 1862. Fort Purbrook is now home to the Peter Ashley Activity Centre, which caters for youth groups and offers a wide range of facilities, including archery, climbing and table tennis, and is occasionally used for craft fairs. (23/80/2a)

HMS Invincible leaving Portsmouth Harbour on 5 April 1982, with large crowds gathered wishing good luck to their loved ones as she sails towards the Falkland Isles to defend British sovereignty against the Argentinians. There is a memorial to the servicemen killed in the war on the wall below where the photographer was standing. A/2/B/401/2)

HMS Hermes returning from the Falklands conflict on 20 July 1982. She was escorted into Portsmouth Harbour by a flotilla of small craft whose crews, along with thousands of other people, were celebrating her safe return.

(DA/2/B/401/1)

The construction of the new Isle of Wight ferry terminal in progress, 1981-2. The terminal is sited in the Camber in Old Portsmouth where there had been a quay for colliers serving the power station. The vehicle ferry service had previously berthed on the other side of the Camber, near East Street.   (65/81)

Portsmouth Power Station, located in Old Portsmouth near the Camber, was demolished in 1983. It originated in the council's decision in 1889 to supply electricity to the ever-increasing population of the city, and generating began on 6 June 1894. The station was bombed on 10 January 1941, and nationalised in 1948.

(LH slides CC190)

In the summer of 1983, 18,356 followers celebrated Portsmouth Football Club's return to Division 2 after seven years. Promotion was at the expense of Southend, who lost 2-0 at Fratton Park. Kevin Dillon and Alan Biley were the goal scorers.

(99/83/12)

On the 3 June 1984 the Queen Mother visited Portsmouth to open officially the D-Day Museum at Southsea. The museum marked an important era of British history, commemorating the battle which began the liberation of western Europe. The operation was called 'Overlord' and is beautifully explained in the museum's main attraction, the 272ft-long embroidery which tells the story of the D-Day landings.   (137/84)

On the 13 October 1984 army bomb-disposal experts were called in to attend an unexploded 500lb bomb which had landed on the Hippodrome Theatre, near Guildhall Square, in a bombing raid in 1941. The incident caused great disappointment as a concert by Bob Hope in the Guildhall had to be cancelled. Everyone within 300 yards had to be evacuated whilst the bomb was being made safe by the Royal Engineers, who had travelled from Chatham, Kent. The remains of the bomb can be seen at the City Museum and Records Office.   (Courtesy of *The News*)

Councillor George Byng, Chairman of the Docks Committee, along with colleagues and councillors, unveiling a sign in February 1984. George Byng Way, which is part of Wharf Road, opened up a new access to the ferryport. The effort, dedication and work that Cllr George Byng put into the new development at the ferryport earned him this accolade.

(45/84/7)

Anchorage Park, photographed here in 1986, was built on the site of Portsmouth Airport. The housing development offered 700 new homes, a supermarket and 50 acres for industry, hence more employment. The estate was designed to reduce the number of houses overlooking another house and to create quiet cul-de-sacs.

(163/86/G32)

In April 1986 Southsea seafront was visited by Princess Diana, who came to open the Sealife Centre. The Centre offers the opportunity to see marine creatures close up. Before it was built, this area catered for families by providing a paddling pool for children and a miniature railway that ran alongside the seafront.

(57/86)

On 13 May 1787, 11 ships sailed from Portsmouth Harbour, led by *HMS Sirius*, to the unknown continent of Australia. Two hundred years later Portsmouth and Australia celebrated the bicentenary. This celebration was attended by Her Majesty The Queen, who was entertained by Aborigine dancers from the Northern Territory

(DA/2/B/44/2)

In 1987 southern England experienced some of the most severe weather conditions this century. Although forecasters predicted high winds, they underestimated the violence of the storm that visited Portsmouth on the 16 October. Winds in excess of 100 mph reaped havoc among many properties and trees, especially along Ladies Mile.

(192/87/C)

HMS Warrior entering Portsmouth Harbour in June 1987. *Warrior* was Britain's first ironclad warship and the most powerful ship of her time when she was launched in 1860. She never fired a shot in anger. (DA/2/B/1381)

The *Trincomalee*, renamed *Foudroyant* in 1897, for decades provided excellent training for schoolchildren in nineteenth-century seamanship. Sadly, in May 1989 the *Foudroyant* left Portsmouth Harbour for Hartlepool, where her restoration is almost complete. (135/87/A12)

Photomontage of the eastern part of Harry Pounds' scrapyard, 1988. This well-known scrapyard was started just after the Second World War at Tipner Magazine. The site became the last resting place for many military vehicles. The construction of the M275 caused problems for the scrapyard, as the motorway divided it in two. (86/1991)

The demolition of Portsdown Park under way early in 1988. Many of the homes in this large housing development suffered from water penetration. No solution could be found and health problems associated with the dampness were affecting the tenants so the council decided to knock it down. Private houses were built on the site.

(PCRO)

The new shopping centre, Cascades, was opened in September 1989 by the Lord Mayor, Councillor Miss Gladys Howard. The centre occupies the car park that was to the rear of Woolworths and C&As, and which had been housing until the blitz of 1940-41. Cascades is the largest indoor shopping centre to open in Portsmouth. (DA/2/B/238)

Andrew Bell, born in Scotland 1753, remembered his schooldays as follows: 'I never went to school without trembling. I could not tell whether I should be flogged or not'. He became a clergyman and in 1797 published a book, *Experiment in Education*. The National School Society was under Bell's care and supported by the Church of England. In 1812 a boys' school, later Bell Street School, was opened in Clarence Street. Its remains can be seen today at the back of Sainsburys. (LH slides BK14)

149

The 'Old Sweet Shop' in Cosham dated back to the seventeenth century. Sadly first one half of the shop was demolished, which resulted in many of the interior features being lost, then the other. All that now remains is the stone falcon which used to surmount the facade. (PMRS)

The Bridge Tavern, at 224 Somers Road, Landport, opened its doors to the public in 1867. The bridge on which the pub was situated used to be Turner's Bridge, and crossed the canal. In 1846-7 the canal bridge was replaced by a rail bridge when the railway was built on the course of the failed canal. (LH slides AL1)

The creation of bunds of chalk from Portsdown Hill, and landfill with domestic refuse around Horsea Island, made way for the building of Port Solent. This new marina, photographed here in 1989, offered 600 units of housing and 1000 berths for boats. The complex was given a range of restaurants, pubs and shops, and the cinema was the first multiscreen to come to Portsmouth. The development has proved very successfull. (DA/2/B/100)

The Duchess of York came to the City Museum and Art Gallery on 13 June 1989, during Museums Year. Her visit included a tour of the corporation buses on display at the rear of the museum. A collection of trolleybuses, corporation buses, etc, is housed at the City of Portsmouth Preserved Transport Depot, which regularly runs and displays the vehicles. (122/89)

On the 11 May 1989 the Bridge Shopping Centre, left, opened its doors to an awaiting crowd, eager to see the new complex. The Bridge Centre was built upon the site where the Co-op department store used to be. Within the complex there is a variety of national and local retailers, also a café area and a large food supermarket. At the back of the centre is a large car park and a petrol station.

(DA/2/B/455)

The Pyramids, a leisure complex with a fun pool with water slide, bar and conference facilities was opened in 1988. It replaced the Rock Gardens Pavilion. Its construction was a council initiative, seeking to promote the success of Southsea as a resort by providing indoor activities for wet days.

(199/88/A11)

1990 – 1999

In 1990 Portsmouth and Duisburg celebrated the fortieth anniversary of the twinning of the two cities, with events in both Portsmouth and Duisburg. Over the forty years there had been a lively programme of visits and exchanges, and these still continue. (96/90:7)

In 1938-9 Portsmouth's Anglican Cathedral was partially extended by Sir Charles Nicholson, but work was halted by the outbreak of the Second World War. Afterwards a number of alternative schemes were discussed but never adopted, until in 1990 work began to 'complete' the cathedral to new designs by Michael Drury based on Nicholson's scheme. Internally the alterations created a much larger nave area. (BE.9)

Sunbathing by South Parade Pier, 1990. (PCM)

Southsea seafront before the crowds arrive, 1990. (Courtesy of Miss Madge Farrant, PCM)

A busy day at the Bridge Centre in Fratton Road, 7 September 1990.

(Courtesy of Miss Madge Farrant, PCM)

After the Gulf War, a service of thanksgiving was held in Guildhall Square, in June 1991.
(96/91: A11)

Lorries disembarking from the Brittany Ferries vessel *Normandie* at the ferryport, summer 1992.

(102/92/AG)

In October 1992, Diana, Princess of Wales, was granted the freedom of the City of Portsmouth. (186/92:G12)

Portsmouth voluntary lifeguards exercising with a coastguard-helicopter, 1993.　(H/83/93)

In 1993 the aisles of the Garrison Church in Old Portsmouth, which was bombed in the Second World War, were re-roofed, as shown in this photograph.　(ARC.AM.32)

Western Portsmouth from the air, about 1995.

(PCM)

1994 was the 800th anniversary of the granting of Portsmouth's first civic charter by Richard I in 1194, and events were held throughout the year to mark the event. The celebrations were launched at the Pyramids in January 1994. (3/94:C5)

The Gala Bingo Club, 1994. The club is to be converted into a mosque for Portsmouth's growing Muslim community. This and the following three pictures were taken by Danny Weinstein as part of a Portsmouth 800 project, realised in the exhibition *Portsmouth, England, 1994.*   (577/1995)

Excitement at Hilsea Lido, 1994.   (Courtesy of Danny Weinstein, 671/1995)

Darren Stares, tattoo artist, 1994.

(Courtesy of Danny Weinstein, 638/1995)

The funfair, Clarence Pier, 1994.

(Courtesy of Danny Weinstein, PCM)

In the 1990s Portsmouth City Council encouraged a greater awareness of healthy living and environmental issues, including recycling schemes, 'no smoking' policies, and environmentally friendly options for city council staff travelling to work. In this photograph we see the winners of the 1994 'Healthy Puddings' award.

(97/94:7)

Omega Street play area, 1994. (89/94:36)

The refurbished Pitt Street Baths reopened in 1994 as a gymnastics centre.

(164/94:B3)

A meeting of Portsmouth Pensioners' Association in the Civic Offices, 1994. (21/94:5)

Heads of state, veterans, and others attended a state banquet in the Guildhall on 4 June 1994 held as part of the events commemorating the fiftieth anniversary of D-Day. Those present included the Queen, Kings Harald of Norway and Albert of Belgium, Presidents Clinton of the USA, Mitterand of France, Walesa of Poland and Kovac of Slovakia, and the prime ministers of Canada, New Zealand and Australia. (83/94:D21)

On Sunday 5 June 1994 an open-air service of commemoration was held on Southsea Common, attended by heads of state, veterans and their families, civic and military dignitaries, and others. The service was followed by a march past by veterans. (85/94:C3)

In 1994, for the second time, sections of the Tour de France cycle race took place in Britain. The 7 July section began and ended in Portsmouth.

(112/94:F18)

Rees Hall (formally the Pier Hotel), one of the University of Portsmouth's student halls of residence, in 1995. In 1996-7 the building was demolished, and a new hall of residence, in a similar style, was built on the site. (ARC.V.9)

The civic carol service in Guildhall Square, December 1995. (124/95:B18)

The Special Olympics National Summer Games (for people with learning difficulties) were held in Portsmouth on 12-19 July 1997. There were a record 2164 competitors, including 120 from overseas. These were medal winners at one of the cycling events, held at the seafront. (PCM)

A view of Charlotte Street, Christmas 1997. Demolition of the Tricorn
Centre was due to start in the summer of 1999.   (F330/6)

The Ministry of Defence sold the Gunwharf site for redevelopment as a housing, leisure, and entertainment area by the Berkeley Group. Demolition of many of the buildings on the site began in 1998, and the foundations of the Millennium Tower are due to be laid in 1999. This picture shows the site in the mid-1990s.

(Courtesy of the University of Portsmouth Photographic Section, PCM)

This is Pia. Who is she talking to? What will she be telling her grandchildren about the Portsmouth of her childhood?

(Courtesy of Mrs Susan Crockford, PCM)